# BLUEPRINTS

## English Key Stage 2
## Teacher's Resource Book

**Jim Fitzsimmons**

**Rhona Whiteford**

**Stanley Thornes (Publishers) Ltd**

# BLUEPRINTS – HOW TO GET MORE INFORMATION

**Blueprints** is an expanding series of practical teacher's ideas books and photocopiable resources for use in primary schools. Books are available for every Key Stage of every core and foundation subject, as well as for an ever-widening range of other primary needs. **Blueprints** are carefully structured around the demands of the National Curriculum but may be used successfully by schools and teachers not following the National Curriculum in England and Wales.
**Blueprints** provide:

- Total National Curriculum coverage
- Hundreds of practical ideas
- Books specifically for the Key Stage you teach
- Flexible resources for the whole school or for individual teachers
- Excellent photocopiable sheets – ideal for assessment, SATs and children's work profiles
- Supreme value.

Books may be bought by credit card over the telephone and information obtained on (0242) 228888. Alternatively, photocopy and return this FREEPOST form to join our mailing list. We will mail you regularly with information on new and existing titles.

Please add my name to the BLUEPRINTS mailing list. *Photocopiable*

Name _____

Address_____

_____

_____

Postcode_____

To: Marketing Services Dept., Stanley Thornes Publishers, FREEPOST (GR 782), Cheltenham, Glos. GL53 1BR

First published in 1992 by:
Stanley Thornes (Publishers) Ltd
Ellenborough House
Wellington Street
CHELTENHAM GL50 1YD
England

Reprinted 1993
Reprinted 1994

A catalogue record for this book is available from the British Library.

ISBN 0–7487–0580–5

Typeset by Tech-Set, Gateshead, Tyne & Wear
Printed and bound in Great Britian at The Bath Press, Avon

# CONTENTS

# INTRODUCTION

## What is *Blueprints: English*?

*Blueprints: English* is a practical teacher resource specifically written to fulfil the requirements of the National Curriculum in English for primary schools. It provides activities for Key Stage 2.

Each aspect of every Attainment Target at every Level is covered in detail with specific activities related to the examples given in the National Curriculum document. It is presented in simple, easy to understand language to help in the planning of programmes of study.

It consists of a Teacher's Resource Book and an accompanying Pupils' Copymaster Book which closely follow the structure of the publication *English in the National Curriculum* (HMSO, 1990).

## The Teacher's Resource Book

The Teacher's Resource Book is arranged in six sections, each corresponding to one of the six Attainment Targets for English. Within each Attainment Target the work is arranged in three sections which relate to work expected of children at Levels 3, 4 and 5. This is the span of attainment that children are expected to achieve by the end of Key Stage 2. Most children are expected to have reached Level 4, only some are likely to have naturally reached Level 5; for this reason the emphasis in this book is on activities in Levels 3 and 4. The Level 5 section is shorter and provides outlines of activities for more advanced children.

Within each section of the book the heading for work in each Attainment Target is a reproduced extract from the Statutory Provision, comprising the Attainment Target title and applicable Statements of Attainment. These have been reproduced with the permission of the Controller of Her Majesty's Stationery Office.

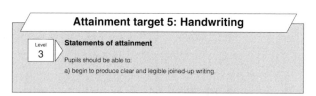

The Teacher's Resource Book will prove an invaluable resource even without the Pupils' Copymasters. You can, in developing your own schemes of work, consult the National Curriculum Key Stage 2 Programmes of Study and then choose activities from *Blueprints: English* to fit those elements on which you are focusing. The coverage of activities is comprehensive and where the use of a secondary resource has been suggested, we have kept these to very well known and easily accessible material.

## The Pupils' Copymaster Book

The Pupils' Copymaster Book provides 124 photocopiable worksheets linked to most of the activities in the Teacher's Resource Book. The work in these copymasters introduces, reinforces and extends the activities and provides usable evidence of the children's experiences. The copymasters may be seen as a resource for teacher assessment in that they provide opportunities to record activities and results in an organised way. You will find notes on how to use the copymasters in this Teacher's Resource Book. The symbol ⤸ appears on Area of study headings to denote that relevant copymasters exist in that section.

Several illustrations which appear in this Teacher's Resource Book can also be photocopied and used in addition to the copymasters (for example page 79).

# ATTAINMENT TARGET 1: Speaking and listening

## Attainment target 1: Speaking and listening

The development of pupils' understanding of the spoken word and the capacity to express themselves effectively in a variety of speaking and listening activities, matching style and response to audience and purpose.

| Level 3 | Statements of attainment | Example |
|---|---|---|
| | Pupils should be able to: | |
| | a) relate real or imaginary events in a connected narrative which conveys meaning to a group of pupils, the teacher or another known adult. | *Tell a story with a beginning, middle and end; recount a series of related incidents that happened at home or in a science activity.* |
| | b) convey accurately a simple message. | *Relay a simple telephone message in role-play or real life; take an oral message to another teacher.* |
| | c) listen with an increased span of concentration to other children and adults, asking and responding to questions and commenting on what has been said. | *Listen to the teacher or to a radio programme on a new topic, then discuss what has been said.* |
| | d) give, and receive and follow accurately, precise instructions when pursuing a task individually or as a member of a group. | *Plan a wall display or arrange an outing together.* |

 **Area of study 1** ## RELATING REAL OR IMAGINARY EVENTS  C1–2

**Purpose**
To provide the opportunity for the children to recognise the beginning, middle and ending of a story and to recount a series of related incidents experienced by them at home or in school.

**Activity 1: Listening to stories**
Listening to and telling stories is sometimes an infrequent event at this stage, often due to pressures from other areas of the curriculum. However it still remains one of the most absorbing and valuable activities for children; one in which they can learn a great deal about the world around them and the world beyond their personal experience. Stories help children to construct their own narrative not only by providing models of structure but by presenting views of imaginary and alternative worlds. They help children to perceive their own world with an increasingly critical eye by making comparisons and trying out language structures of greater complexity and colour. Vocabulary is widened by appreciation of its use and good stories present language as a powerful medium which can entertain, inform, persuade, amuse, shock and horrify. Children learn to love experimenting with the power of language. 'It's how you tell 'em!' and story telling is no exception in the drama stakes. Stories can be told from memory or read, and either way they can be made to capture the attention, develop concentration and fire the imagination, perhaps because of the element of live drama and audience involvement which storytelling weaves into a special magic all of its own.

1

Care must be taken when selecting material as content varies in quality even though there is a vast array to choose from these days. Involve the children in this process to develop their critical faculty and involve them in constructive dialogue. Examine what attracts them to a particular book in the first place. Is it the cover picture, the title, the characters, the fact that the story is on TV, the fact that friends have read it or the action of the story ascertained from illustrations or a quick read?

### Activity 2: Re-telling stories

To encourage discussion about story structure, read simple stories to the children and ask them to re-tell them. Alternatively the children can choose a story they know and try to re-tell that. You can work in small groups to provide a smaller audience for less confident children or to give greater opportunity for discussion afterwards. Encourage careful listening and then get the audience to ascertain whether any part has been missed out. This will be fairly easy with a well-known story but will need careful discussion to decide if part of an unknown story is missing or in the wrong order. The listeners can question the story-teller about that part of the story which does not make sense for some reason. To review what has been heard is a valuable skill but, in this case, must be done sensitively so that the storyteller is not discouraged. Make sure everyone has a chance to be the story-teller in a situation that suits their personality and take this opportunity to use the exercise for a contribution to the child's on-going assessment.

### Activity 3: Analysing stories

After reading a simple story or watching a story video, discuss it with the children, trying to identify the beginning, the middle and the end. Talk about how the story started. How were the characters introduced? How did the children know where the action took place? Try to identify the series of events leading up to the start of the action or adventure. Did something wonderful happen or did something go disastrously wrong? Did the arrival of one of the characters create a difficult situation which necessitated some sort of urgent action? The middle part of the story usually involves a journey, a struggle or a quest and is often the main event of the story, while the end is where the difficulties are overcome and order restored.

Most of the traditional stories can be analysed in this way and the children very quickly come to recognise the different parts. This sort of discussion on a regular basis will help the children to organise their thoughts when writing their own stories.

As a class activity, organise the children into three groups. Give one group the task of producing the beginning of a story, the second group the middle and the third group an ending. You can agree upon a set of characters at the onset. The length of each part will depend upon the ability of the children, but get them to either appoint a spokesperson or speak in turns to describe their ideas to the rest of the class. As each part is produced independently, the results are often hilarious. Puppets can also be used to tell the finished

story and this will help link each of the parts through the characters involved. Another benefit of using puppets is that shy children are often encouraged to project themselves in a way they would not if asked to speak under normal classroom circumstances.

As an extension of this activity, organise the children into small groups and allow them to further organise their group to think up a beginning, middle and an end to an adventure for an agreed set of characters. Ask them to decide how they can mime the actions of their story. This will encourage much group discussion about the sorts of actions they consider appropriate to help interpret and enhance the narrative. The actions will also serve to reinforce the continuity of the story-line and at the same time encourage recall and development of memory.

### Activity 4: Ways to begin a story

Ask the children how most stories begin and they will most likely reply, 'Once upon a time'. Encourage them to think of some other openings, possibly involving the time of day or the time of the week:

'It was a beautiful sunny morning …'
'Just after lunch time …'
'It was late at night …'
'On Monday I am going to visit …'
'Yesterday I saw a …'
'Tomorrow I will …'
'Last night the wind was blowing so hard that …'

The place or location of the story is essential to the plot and setting the scene is a good way to start:

'I was in the garden when …'
'I was walking down the road when it happened.'
'They were deep in the forest…'

2

Finally ask the children to think about beginnings that set the mood or tone of the story: fear, amusement, adventure or mystery.

'The old, dark house stood silently in the moonlight. As I reached the steps that led to the front door I thought I saw a strange light shining in through the window. I was just about to climb the steps when the door began to creak open. I looked up and there, right in front of me was …'

Ask the children to decide what sort of story they want to tell and, working in pairs or groups, they can discuss suitably atmospheric openings.

### Activity 5: What happens in the story?

Discuss the opening actions and locations. Talk about suitable exciting locations such as a castle, a cave, a haunted house, a fairground, a strange land, the moon and wherever the children can suggest. Go on to discuss the possibilities for adventure at any of the locations and choose one of the children's suggestions to explore in detail. You can suggest extra details which the children may not have thought of. For example, if a castle is chosen, have the children thought of the following features: dungeons, battlements, the torture chamber, ghosts, suits of armour, old maps, treasure, secret doors and passages? Use one of these elements to feature in an opening action.

Talk about the characters who are in the story. Do the children themselves feature? Is there a good character or an evil one from whom they have to escape? The children can have as many characters as they choose.

Go on to decide about the main action of the plot and you can start by discussing the different events the children have actually experienced, such as: going on a picnic, visiting a place of interest, going to a football match, getting lost, losing something special. At the same time try to develop creativity by asking them to imagine what it would be like to visit another planet, look for lost treasure in a cave or underwater, or to be captured by aliens. See also, *Blueprints: Writing* for further ideas.

### Activity 6: Ways to end a story

Read the endings of a few well-known stories and discuss with the children how they felt about them. Were they satisfying or unnerving? Talk about what makes a good or a bad ending. Should the ending always be happy or is it better for some stories to end sadly? To illustrate the need for an ending that is satisfactory to the plot, read a story and at a very exciting point stop and say, 'The end!' and watch the children's reactions. This should help them to realise the importance of a good ending. Another way is to read the story up to a turning point in the action and then ask the children to discuss in small groups how they feel the plot will continue and how the story will end. Let each group report back to the class and then read the actual end to the story. No doubt this will stimulate further discussion of how right or wrong some were in their predictions. The children may actually prefer their own ending to that of the author.

Make a list of as many different endings as possible and keep them for reference. Start them off with a few examples:

'When I woke up I was in my own bed at home. Had it all been a dream?'

'Just then a voice shouted, "Cut." The filming was over for another day.'

'And the last we saw of him he was shouting, "You haven't seen the last of me. I'll be back to get you!" as he disappeared over the hill.'

See *Blueprints Writing* for more ways to end a story.

### Activity 7: Concentration

Write out a number of simple nursery rhymes and poems and split each into a beginning, middle and end, on separate pieces of paper. Start off with well-known rhymes. Using three children per poem, give them the parts of their verse and ask them to arrange them in the correct order, then read them to the rest of the class. This will require concentration from the performers and the listeners, particularly if the poems are relatively unknown to them.

### Activity 8: Tell the story

Make a set of cards with simple illustrations showing people involved in a variety of activities. You can use pictures cut from old magazines or books. The set will need to be in three groups. One group should show events or actions which will most likely begin a story, such as people loading a boat. Another group should show exciting events such as an avalanche, a storm or a race. The third group should show a series of outcomes or possible endings such as a boat docking, a race ending, a party or an ambulance driving off. Colour code the sets, then shuffle up the cards. The children can take one from each set. Organise the children into groups. They then have to tell a story to the rest of the group based on the activities on their cards.

### Copymasters

Use **copymaster 1** (Storyboard) to help the children plan their stories. Use each of the labelled boxes to plot in note form the various components of a story, which the children can then tell to the class or the group. Such models as this provide a starting point and a focus for the imagination. Do let the children use the sheets as rough notes which can be altered as the discussion proceeds and as they plan, review and amend.

Use **copymaster 2** (News report). The children look at the picture on the sheet and have to draw a picture of what happened next. They can take it in turns to tell the other children in the group what happens.

**Area of study 2**

# CONVEYING A SIMPLE MESSAGE

C3

### Purpose

To provide situations which allow children to convey messages to other teachers, adults or other children within their group or class.

### Activity 1: Conveying messages in role play situations

Although children at this stage will not have access to a home corner in school, role play or acting out real life and imaginary situations still features strongly in their private play and this can be harnessed to advantage for the purposes of speaking and listening.

At this stage the children will respond to play situations which form part of topic work. For example if you are doing work on communications you could set up a mini telephone exchange in a corner of the room with several toy or old telephones. The children may have sets of hand radios and intercoms which they can bring from home and these can be used to communicate from different parts of the school building. For this area of study give the children a series of messages to pass on, the accuracy of which can be assessed by making it into a version of Chinese Whispers. Finances permitting, let the children use the school telephone to ring some of the Operator services so that they can experience the formal language style. They can then incorporate this into the telephone exchange play.

As part of a topic on communications you may want to include the work of the emergency services, all of which depend on highly efficient communications, the passing on of messages. You may be able to arrange for the children to visit one of the communications control centres or a station. In both cases the children will hear a formalised language in use when messages are passed and a very casual, colloquial language on other occasions. With your encouragement, they will be able to incorporate it into their play in the classroom. Notice the language conventions used in radio communications by the officers and those used by the operators to the public. Can the children identify any much used phrases, such as 'Over', used at the end of a message? Write a short play or work out an improvisation with the children about an accident and include the telephone exchange and the emergency controls, and some of the emergency services' officers. You might like to include some members of the public who, in the panic situation, do not pass on the information clearly.

Other situations which could be developed into play or acting opportunities where conveying a message accurately is part of the action include:

- a restaurant where orders for meals are taken
- a newspaper reporter passing on a scoop to the office

- a taxi cab control passing on locations to drivers
- air traffic control
- the coast guard.

In the last three examples you could set up models using the children's toy cars and road mats or a model coastline with cardboard box cliffs and rocks.

### Activity 2: Conveying messages to another adult in school

Start off with very simple messages conveying one idea or action, such as, 'It's an indoor playtime.' This is usually enough for the verbal memory and confidence of many children even at this stage. As the children gain confidence the messages can become more complex, for example, 'Mr Friend says it's an indoor playtime. The whole school is coming to your room and you are on duty.' Later on the message can be in the form of a question which needs a reply so the children can pass two messages.

The taking of messages forms an essential part of the efficiency of everyday life in school and, when you are busy, it is easy to pick competent children to take messages. Have confidence yourself and try to pick a less able child who really needs the practice. Keep a list of messengers on the wall to record who has had this essential experience and to give the children a sense of achievement and anticipation. A more confident friend can always accompany a messenger who lacks confidence or memory, but the friend should have instructions not to speak unless the messenger asks for help. Far from time-wasting, this activity is an essential part of the development of speaking and listening.

For extra practice enlist the help of a parent helper in a message passing game. The parent can be seated outside the room. Together you can devise messages and replies and each adult can assess the accuracy of the message when it is delivered and give the appropriate reply for the child to take back. Make this as enjoyable an activity as possible, to develop the children's confidence. Emphasise the importance of clear diction and audibility and always get the child to repeat the message before he/she goes. This seems to fix it in the mind.

These simple activities will help memory training and recall, provided they are carried out in a fun way with the emphasis on encouragement and enjoyment. Taking messages can help develop a sense of importance and reliability as the children come to realise that the messages conveyed have to be accurate in order to be useful.

### Activity 3: Conveying messages to different people

Ask the children if they have different ways of talking to different groups of people. Do they know the difference between dialect speech, slang and proper English? Try to find different examples of these for one set of things, for example, food. Do they think one of these types of speech is more appropriate for one type of listener? Try out one simple message such as, 'Tea is ready', for a variety of listeners: a parent, a friend, a baby, an old person, a teacher, an adult or child they do not know well and a TV star or character they admire. Discuss situations with the children and try to identify when they would use one type of language or another and try to identify those phrases which might be acceptable in one situation but totally unsuitable in another.

### Activity 4: Passing messages in different areas of the curriculum

There will be times when, working in different areas of the curriculum, the children will need to pass on information and instructions to other children. They may be instructions for performing tasks or directions for obtaining materials. Very often children gain far more understanding from explaining a task to another child and the importance of this activity should not be underestimated. The messenger can gain a sense of worth from helping a peer and some children find it easier to understand instructions from peers and feel more relaxed in a shared experience of this kind.

## Copymasters

Use **copymaster 3** (Telephone calls) to encourage children to think about what they want to convey in a message. Each of the pictures shows a different situation requiring a message. Photocopy one sheet for each child in a group and one extra to be cut up to make a set of cards for use by the group. The children take it in turns to shuffle the cards and choose one. They have a few minutes to think of what they are going to say and then they have to make a telephone call with an old telephone. If you have two such phones one child can be the enquirer while the other can be the shop or the service required. This will encourage a two-way conversation which will help the flow of dialogue. With practice the children can become quite proficient. The sheet can provide a record of the activity if the children colour in the picture showing which situation they were involved with. The space at the bottom can be used for making short notes of the type of questions they wish to ask or of the information they wish to convey. If the children are unable to do this, simply colouring in their picture will record their experience.

# LISTENING AND COMMENTING

Area of study 3

C4

## Introduction

Children should now be able to listen for longer periods and still maintain concentration. They should have experience of listening to a variety of subjects delivered in different ways: talking to peers, adults and sometimes in a non-reciprocal situation, such as listening to the radio or tapes. This is vitally important for all areas of the curriculum as new topics are introduced and, as the Programme of Study suggests, they will need to ask questions, work in groups, explain and present ideas and, in this area of study, respond to questions and comment on what has been said.

## Purpose

To help the children listen with increased concentration and respond appropriately.

## Materials needed

Tape recorder or record-player and recorded music, prose or poetry; a copy of the *Radio Times* and programme notes for selected programmes.

## Activity 1: Listen to a radio programme

Bearing in mind other curricular needs, plan to listen to BBC programmes which offer new topics. It is important to establish a habit of listening to the spoken word and listening with the knowledge that what is being heard is new and interesting, and you may want to know more. Prime the children before the programme with a positive encouragement to listen carefully, 'This is really very interesting. We'll talk about it after the programme.' Then they are prepared to discuss it afterwards.

Ask the children for their opinions of the topic and the programme and what, if anything, they would like to know more about. They can take it in turns to lead the discussion after the programme.

## Activity 2: Science and Maths

Whenever a new topic is introduced in these and other curricular areas it is always good practice to question the children to see if they have understood before going on. Make it a little more qualitative as well as knowledge-based by asking them which parts they

enjoyed most and why, so that they begin to get an idea of their own preferences and skills.

## Activity 3: Listening to music

Listen to short pieces at a time of a variety of different styles of music and discuss how it makes the children feel and which they like or dislike.

## Activity 4: CDT tasks

This discipline needs careful discussion in the planning stages and usually several reviews of the situation. This still needs the sort of group discussion where members say, 'What do you think of that?' 'What shall we do about this?' 'I like this, what do you think?' 'That's a good idea but I think we need a … as well.'

## Activity 5: Children as teacher

Get the children to introduce a new topic or idea to the others. You can explain the idea to one child who can then do the same to a small group or an individual. You can then listen to see how well they have assimilated the information and guide if necessary.

## Copymasters

Use **copymaster 4** (I've been listening) for the children to make notes after a discussion. They can record the topic, the method of dissemination and the main points in which they are interested.

6

# FOLLOWING AND LEADING

C5

## Introduction

Children should already have had some practice at following precise instructions but, at this level, they should be given experience of tasks requiring greater concentration, accuracy and responsibility involving a planning element. They should also be allowed to try the leadership role and give instructions to others. Do not forget that the Programme of Study recommends that we should emphasise the importance of clear diction and audibility.

## Purpose

To give practice working in a group situation as the leader or a group member at a greater level of accuracy.

## Activity 1: Planning a wall display

As part of the discussion on a new topic the children should have had enough experience by now to contribute ideas for wall displays, and it is useful to do this on a more organised level so that the topic can be seen as a whole and the more important parts emphasised by a large picture or a model. Try to get the children to understand that such a display is both a record of their work and a way of communicating the information to others as well as looking attractive. When it comes to the actual production of work and its display, give the children the opportunity to lead a small group and see that the original plan is being carried out. See *Bright ideas for display*, published by Scholastic by the same authors.

## Activity 2: Planning a trip

This is something very exciting for the children to be involved in and will surely spark off much enthusiasm as well as involving them in decisions and learning the logical process of planning.

## Copymasters

Use **copymaster 5** (Planning an outing) for this activity. It lists in question form the usual points to be considered when planning a trip. It can be filled in by the children as part of the discussion or used as a guide to the discussion if enlarged to A3 size so that a group can see it clearly. It can also be used as an information sheet for parents.

## Activity 3: Domestic jobs

There are usually many daily jobs to be done in a classroom such as preparing writing materials, milk, painting things, science equipment and caring for pets and plants. Instruct one group at the beginning of the week and let them instruct the following group but you will need to monitor the situation, particularly where living things are concerned.

## Attainment target 1: Speaking and listening

The development of pupils' understanding of the spoken word and the capacity to express themselves effectively in a variety of speaking and listening activities, matching style and response to audience and purpose.

| Level 4 | Statements of attainment | Example |
|---|---|---|
| | Pupils should be able to: | |
| | a) give a detailed oral account of an event, or something that has been learned in the classroom, or explain with reasons why a particular course of action has been taken. | *Report on a scientific investigation, or the progress of a planned group activity, to another group or the class.* |
| | b) ask and respond to questions in a range of situations with increased confidence. | *Guide other pupils in designing something; conduct an interview on a radio programme devised with other pupils.* |
| | c) take part as speakers and listeners in a group discussion or activity, expressing a personal view and commenting constructively on what is being discussed or experienced. | *Draft a piece of writing, with others, on a word processor; contribute to the planning and implementation of a group activity.* |
| | d) participate in a presentation. | *Describe the outcome of a group activity; improvise a scene from a story or poem or of the pupils' own devising.* |

# DETAILED ORAL ACCOUNTS

## Purpose
To encourage the children to give detailed oral accounts of an event or something learned in the classroom, giving reasons for particular courses of action.

## Activity 1: Presentation
Discuss with the children how they would like to present their account of their chosen activity or event. They may decide to work as a group and elect one person as spokesperson. Alternatively they may prefer to each take one aspect of the presentation, and give their own account in turn. The subjects to be presented can be of the children's own choosing, and can include any work they are involved in from any area of the curriculum. If the children have taken part in any sporting event or an activity or competition of any kind, use this as the starting point for their presentation, and form them into small discussion groups. Give them time to organise their ideas and go from group to group in order to help them do this. By careful questioning you can encourage them to think about the reasons why they pursued a particular course of action and encourage them to include these reasons when they give their account. Careful thought must be given to the audience. At first the children may be more comfortable speaking to a small group, to the teacher or another known adult but, with practice, the audience can be widened to give them a greater variety and to help develop their confidence.

## Activity 2: A scientific investigation
When the children first start to think about presenting an account of a scientific investigation to another group or the rest of the class, they will need to think about the reasons for undertaking the investigation. What did they need to find out? This should be stated at the beginning. Then they will need to say what materials they required and whether there were any difficulties in obtaining them. They can then talk about how they started their investigation, how they set up the equipment, whether any special conditions had to be created and any difficulties they had in doing this. They can then go on to talk about how the investigation progressed and whether anything happened to make them change their course of action. They can highlight their account with illustrations or by using the experiment itself to point out what went wrong and what they did to rectify any mistakes or changes. The final part of the account should include presentation of any conclusions reached as a result of the investigation and the audience can be encouraged to ask questions.

## Activity 3: A sporting event
If the children have reached the final of a sporting event, they can be encouraged to give an account of this to the rest of the school, especially if they are successful and can show off the trophy or prize at an assembly. The start of the account can be to tell the audience how they reached the final, and which child or children were involved. If the sporting event is a familiar sport or activity it may not be necessary to go into too much detail as to how the points were acquired to win, but if the sport is little known it will be useful to give details of scoring. The account can be illustrated by bringing in any special equipment needed for the sport and any demonstration of particular skills or prowess will also help to enhance the account. Then the battle for supremacy in the final can be described with details of individual efforts to score or defend, the final outcome being the winning or losing of the trophy. If the event is of local importance the result may have featured in the local newspaper or, if it is of regional importance, on local radio or television. The account could be concluded with a recording being played of this together with a display of photographs. Encourage the use of visual aids whenever possible.

## Activity 4: Topic work
An account of individual topic work or interests is a good subject for individual accounts presented to the class or small groups. The children can start off by talking about what started their interest in the subject. They can then go on to say how they found the information they needed, where they went to and whether they had to write to any particular organisations, whether they had to join any of these organisations, what benefits they have derived from membership and whether this has encouraged their interest and put them in contact with other people who share the same interest. As before, encourage the children to illustrate their talk with any writing or illustrations they have done. An example of this could be a topic on birds. The children could talk about how they found lots of books on birds, how they wrote to the Royal Society for the Protection of Birds and joined their organisation, how they got in touch with a local ornithologists club, how they became interested in bird spotting by meeting members of that club and how various skills were passed on in order to help them observe birds more closely. They might have learnt about the right sort of foods to put out to attract certain species, ways of constructing bird-tables which ensure that the birds are safe from cats, the best locations to observe particular birds and ways of recognising them from their silhouettes in the sky.

## Activity 5: Planning an assembly
Sometimes children can be involved in the planning of a class assembly and they can be encouraged to give a detailed account of the planning after the assembly has been performed. They can be encouraged to make notes from when the subject of the assembly was chosen and talk about which aspects were decided upon for inclusion. They can talk about the writing of the assembly, the allocation of parts, the creation of visual aids and art work to illustrate it and any problems encountered in translating their ideas into practice. They can talk about any compromises they had to make

**Visit museums to stimulate imagination**

or any changes in their original ideas and why they had to make these changes.

**Activity 6: Imaginary accounts**
In certain subjects the children can be encouraged to use their imagination in order to put themselves in a situation and then provide reasons for a particular course of action. An example of this might be for a child to imagine that he or she was a character from history such as King Henry VIII and to explain why he had six wives and why two of them had their heads chopped off. They could also imagine that they were children alive during the reign of Queen Victoria and try to picture what life would have been like during those times, especially if they had to work in a coal mine or a factory. There are many National Trust properties which take parties of school children for a day and give them activities designed to recreate, as far as possible, the atmosphere of life below-stairs in a large house. Also many heritage museums are now designed in such a way as to really involve visitors in the exhibits and, through the use of actors and sound effects, are much more effective in the recreation of past times. A visit to such an establishment will provide a really useful starting point for the children's accounts.

**Activity 7: Imaginary accounts based on everyday life**
An extension of the previous activity is to take everyday situations and ask the children to give reasons or an explanation for a particular course of action. One such situation might be for them to imagine that they have just been asked by their parents to explain why they have arrived home late from school. The children can be encouraged to say what had caused them to be late. Had they been involved in an accident? Had something happened to them to cause them to be late? Maybe they had stopped to help someone or some creature in distress or maybe they had just stopped somewhere to play football. The class could be split into groups and each group should be encouraged to provide a different reason for their lateness.

**Copymasters**
Use **copymaster 6** (Reasons) as a sheet for making notes for their detailed accounts. The different sections can be used either for step-by-step descriptions of the stages of a scientific experiment, for the details of the progress of a group activity or for highlighting the reasons why a particular course of action was taken.

9

Area of study 2

# QUESTIONS

 C7–8

## Introduction
Children at this stage may already have had quite a bit of experience at working in groups of various sizes and this can provide a range of experiences, not least of which is assuming a responsibility for working without the direct help of an adult for part of the time. They are often motivated by each other's enthusiasm for a task, peer pressure being paramount! They also respond to each other's language, possibly because it is just that, a shared language style and is more relaxed than that used by a teacher or another adult. And they are stimulated by each other's ideas. Indeed brainstorming is a technique used to effect by adults. Throughout life we need to give and take instructions, question and respond, and collaborate with others in a variety of situations. Children can learn to challenge each other's ideas in a constructive way and they can learn to work together towards a shared goal, provided they are given plenty of experience and help by adults who intervene compassionately.

## Purpose
To give the children opportunities to ask and to respond to questions with increased confidence.

## Materials needed
Rough paper, card, pens, tape recorder, TV and video.

## Activity 1: Guiding others in designing something
This is a group situation which needs a definite leadership element, group co-operation and precise use of language to question and to respond in order to achieve the goal.

It can be tackled in two ways. You can use one or two children at this level to guide children who are younger and at an earlier level. Using two leaders means they can be mutually supportive socially and pool their ideas. Alternatively, you can construct a situation where children of the same level can agree to take on the two roles. In order to do this you will need to organise the children into groups made up of two pairs, one set to guide and the other to be guided. They will need to agree about mutually complementary roles and general ground rules and they will need a goal. In this situation the children are trying out the roles and this may make them think carefully about the language used in each situation.

Possible design projects could be: the layout of equipment for PE in the hall, an obstacle course, the classroom layout, a garden design for a children's garden, a garden design to encourage animals to visit, an adventure park, a board game, an advertisement, a useful machine or a school uniform design.

Working with all the children you can discuss the type of questions that the leaders will need to ask to make the workers think about their design. There are a number of general questions whatever the project: What is needed? What is its purpose? Who will use it? When will it be used? Where is it to be made? Where will it be sited? What materials are needed to make it? Have we got them? How much will they cost? Who will make it? How long will it take?

Use **copymaster 7** (Checklist) to help with this activity. You can photocopy this at A3 size for the class to use as a general guide or the sheets can be used by the leaders in each group who can add their own questions in the space provided.

As each group's project begins you will have to observe them closely and intervene, if necessary, to guide the children to ask quite specific questions, for example, 'Why have you chosen red for that?' or 'Does the lever need to be as long as that or will it work as well if it is shorter?' With practice the children will become confident enough to respond positively to being questioned. You can help them to listen carefully, consider the suggestion and respond appropriately and, of course, politely. At this level they should be aware of many dangers but will need you to advise and it is important that they use a variety of reference sources whenever the need arises.

It is vital that the children understand that their role as questioner is not as an interrogator, nor are they to deliberately find fault. Rather they are enquiring in a spirit of mutual co-operation, spotting difficulties the workers are too busy to notice in the flurry of activity.

## Activity 2: Conducting an interview
This is a slightly more formal question and answer situation where people get together for the purpose of asking and responding to questions on a specific topic. There is also the added dimension of a formal audience who are there to be interested, informed and/or entertained. An interview has an element of performance and because of this, the added dimension of some degree of stress.

Start off by watching a selection of different types of interviews on television. Daytime TV and the frequent news bulletins offer a selection of material in the middle of the day. You can video a short selection, perhaps including varied items such as interviews with: pop stars or cult figures, sports persons after the 'event', the man in the street asked for a quick opinion, people involved in a disaster, consumers asked about a product, political figures on news programmes or interesting people, for example on *Wogan*.

You could also compile a tape of short radio interviews including: the quick interview in between records on a music programme, the in-depth interview such as *Desert Island Discs* or the telephone call-in.

Ask the children to work in groups and compile a list of real-life subjects they would like to hear about from other children. Their list might include the following subjects: a favourite hobby, sport or interest; feelings about a real-life event such as a wedding, birthday or birth; a friend; a great/disastrous holiday; their country, religion or culture; their family; a fantastic place to have fun or visit; graffiti and vandalism; bullying; something strange that happened to them.

Organise them into small groups of two, three or four. Ask them to pick a subject they would like to hear more about and then to write down or think of six questions they want to ask. One of the group has to be the person being interviewed and another the interviewer. They can draw straws or use some other

fair chance means of selection, but do not do this until they have thought of the questions. At first let them conduct the interview in their group until they have gained confidence and later open this to a class performance, possibly changing the subjects and the performers.

Again working in groups, let the children plan out a radio programme of whatever type they like and include in it either one of their earlier interviews or a co-opted member of the class, possibly with specialist knowledge about, for example, skateboarding, wildlife or *Neighbours*. An easy programme to start with is a pop music programme with short interviews between records. To give the children a taste for production try restricting the music to short snatches and limiting the interviews to three so that they can be recorded and listened to in a relatively short time.

After the children have had a chance to speak about real-life events and personal experiences, they would enjoy doing the exercise again but this time based on an imaginary experience.

When planning the programme the children will have to consider the following questions: What is the programme to be about? Who is going to listen to it? How long will it last? What items should be included in it? Who will write the script? Who will be the presenters? Do we need incidental music or an opening theme? Do we need a title?

11

### Activity 3: Role play

Have a brainstorming session with the children and try to think of as many situations, real and imaginary, where questions are posed and answers given. You may come up with some of the following:

*Real situations* – in a shop, asking about a product; searching for a person, place or lost object; lost, asking for help (which people to approach?); finding out how a toy or game works; police questioning a suspect; a teacher questioning a child about an incident; ambulance personnel questioning a patient about where he is injured; finding out how a machine works (computer, calculator, TV, video); finding out from other children or the teacher how to do domestic jobs in the classroom; playing games involving questions of choice (Grannie's garden); finding out what a toddler wants to play with; finding out what an old person has forgotten on the shopping list; talking to a new pupil from another country about their past.

*Imaginary situations* – asking a pet what it thinks about its owner; asking a zoo animal what it thinks about captivity; questioning an alien about its home; asking a Roman/Elizabethan/Victorian child about his/her life.

Let the children work in pairs or fours, pick a situation that appeals and act out the various roles. If working in fours, two can act and two observe and comment. In order to make this effective the children should immediately assume the role given and pretend to be that person. A certain posture may be needed and some small props such as hats will help. It may be helpful to give the children in each group a starter question for one of the roles. They may also notice that the various roles will use different language styles. These sorts of activities are great fun and the children will soon learn confidence in the excitement of the moment. Make the whole activity fairly casual with the emphasis on probable conversation and not the excellence of acting.

## Activity 4: Games

The following is a selection of short games which rely on questions and answers and can be played on a regular basis to inspire the children to think about why and how they ask questions and how they answer them.

*Game 1 Give me three*    Think of a number of interesting topics and write these on the board. The children can work in pairs and are to think of three to six questions about the topic of their choice. Everyone says their question in turn and those deemed by the children to be most thoughtful and intriguing are written on the board to be discussed later.

*Game 2 Tricky ones*    The game is simply to think of the most unusual questions which do not seem to have an answer but will promote discussion, for example:
'Is a hole a cave?' 'What is darkness?' 'Are people in Australia upside down?'

Write these questions in speech bubbles and put them around the room for children to ponder on.

*Game 3 Quiz time*    Any type of quiz on whatever subject is a question and answer game. Play in teams or with a 'guest panel' and let the children think up the questions on the subject, using reference books if necessary.

*Game 4 Cartoon speech bubbles*    Use **copymaster 8** (Lip-reading) and ask small groups of children to work together to decide what each of the pairs of characters are saying to each other.

*Game 5 Piggy-in-the-middle*    Work in groups or as a class and put one child in a 'hot seat' to answer questions about themselves. The child who is 'it' has to answer without using the pronoun 'I' and can use their name instead if they wish. This is surprisingly difficult. For those who are good, limit the questions to six to give others a chance.

13

*Game 6 Antiques road show*     Provide a number of old artefacts which are unusual but not too obscure. Keep the name and use a secret to all but one 'expert' or a small panel of 'experts' and invite the audience to ask ten questions about each object to try to discover the answer. Change the 'expert' after each object and encourage them to give more than a 'yes' or 'no' answer. By setting the example yourself, provide an answer which gives encouragement if the guess is warm: 'Yes it is used to hold something, but it's not food.' Objects could include items such as dolly peg, a flint lighter, an identity card, a miner's lamp, a candle holder, a flint arrow head.

*Game 7 What's my line?*     One child is 'on' and assumes the role of an historical figure, a pop star, a professional person or a TV character and must do a short mime to represent this. The rest of the class or group can ask a total of 20 questions to try to discover the role. The one who is 'on' can answer questions and can give verbal clues.

*Game 8 Call my bluff*     Give groups of four children a selection of four unusual words (nouns are good to start with) and the correct definitions. They have to think of two incorrect but plausible definitions for each word. Get the class together and organise a panel game like the TV version, with two opposing teams trying out the words on each other. Let them make their own 'True' and 'Bluff' cards. More able children can look up their own words in the dictionary.

*Game 9 Pork pies*     One child thinks of a silly object, which is then known as the 'pork pie'. Working in pairs or small groups, he/she is then questioned about it in a light-hearted manner. The questioners must use the words 'pork pie' in every question: How big is your pork pie? Is your pork pie alive? Does your pork pie make a noise?

*Game 10 Family favourites*     Let the children work in small groups for this game so that they can really get down to talking about their families. They have to think of a question each member of their family is always asking with monotonous regularity, for example:
*Brother:* 'Where's my tea?'
*Mum:* 'Where have you been? Have you been good?'
*Dad:* 'How's my favourite boy?'
Include friends and self in the discussion. Get together as a class and compare findings to see if there is any question common to a particular family member. You could display these as 'The things Mums ask us!'

*Game 11 Way out!*     Get together in small groups to think up sets of three bizarre, yet funny situations, such as: drinking a gallon of cold custard, jumping in jam up to the neck, being squeezed by a slimy squid, etc. Put the groups together in pairs and let them fire the sets of situations at individuals in the opposite group and ask 'Which would you rather do?' The idea is to think of the one situation of the three which appeals most and give a reason for it. It is great fun!

# WORKING TOGETHER

## Introduction

Working with others can be both stimulating and difficult. It can provide a range of experience socially, emotionally and intellectually. However, in order for the children to get maximum benefit, you will need to organise such situations carefully so that the more confident group members do not take on too much of a controlling role to the detriment of others. It is useful to give formalised roles to the group members to provide a basis for the collaboration, for example a chairperson, a secretary and a time keeper. You will need to supervise carefully and intervene if necessary to aid collaboration, help construct arguments, settle arguments, provide a reference and to help the group to keep the goal in mind.

The children need experience of working in groups of different sizes but, to establish good working practice, a pair is very useful. It is easier to learn rules of collaboration, to construct arguments and points of view and to take turns to express them in a pair situation. With regular practice they can learn to try to see things from another's point of view. Encourage them to ask what other group members think, need, want or feel. If new ideas muddle or upset, try to get them to see it as a challenge to be met. Encourage them not to be afraid to question what they do not understand, to criticise and if necessary alter ideas. Gradually increase the size of the groups but maintain regular experience in smaller groups to reinforce confidence for those who need this.

Equally as important as the mechanics of the group is the reason for the group's establishment. Children need a clearly defined purpose for their activities and the following should serve to inspire some fruitful group work.

## Purpose

To give the children experience of working in a group and the confidence to express a personal view and comment constructively on the project in hand.

## Materials needed

Paper, pens and word processor.

## Activity 1: Composing writing together

First of all a purpose for writing is needed and, closely associated with this, is the intended audience.

You will probably have given the purpose of the writing as the reason for establishing the group in the first place and this can be the first item for discussion, the group asking themselves such questions as: Is the writing intended to entertain, inform, direct, warn or what else? Will it take the form of a story, an advertisement, a poster or a letter? What age is the audience (younger children, peers, adults, old people)? What style does the writing need to have? Should it be formal, funny or serious? How long does it need to be? How is it to be produced (by hand or on a word processor)? How is it to be presented? Will it be read aloud or read by the audience?

Once these questions have been decided, the group may find it useful to decide on different roles such as: typist/scribe, chairperson, spelling checker. They can change roles if necessary and, in any case, this would give a spread of experience in the activity. The simplest procedure is to make notes on paper as a result of brainstorming and then write a first draft. This can then be read by the group who can ask themselves if the writing is suitable for what they intended. Does it say the things they wanted to say and, if not, how can it be changed? The formula: draft, read, review, amend, is a good basis for self questioning. To provide a model of how to work in this situation, you can offer suggestions on format, sentence construction, vocabulary etc. Encourage positive thinking and constructive comment and praise. Children respond just as well, if not better, to praise from peers as from the teacher. Get them into the habit of asking each other what they think and why.

Encourage quiet discussion, courteous behaviour, clear diction and audibility.

After the work is done it is useful to review the task and the method of working and ask of each other: Was it successful and, if so, why? What problems arose and how were they resolved? Has anything been learnt which will make the job easier next time?

## Activity 2: Planning a group activity

This should be a popular and stimulating task especially if you allow the children to plan an activity which is for them or has a direct bearing on their daily life. Suitable activities could be: a trip for the class or for another, younger class in school; an entertainment for the school, a younger group, parents or local old people; a party; a games lesson; arranging the domestic jobs in

the classroom; designing a quiet or private area in the classroom; designing a science or craft area.

The same method of working can be used as for Activity 1 and the same process of draft, read, review and amend can be used as the plans are formed or committed to a written form. Questions for the group to ask itself will probably be: What is the activity? Who will it involve? Where will it be? When will it be? Will we need equipment? Will we need special clothes? Will we need food? Will we need transport? How much will this cost? Where will the money come from? What jobs are involved? Which group members will do which job?

See **copymaster 5** (Planning an outing) which can be used as a checklist for a trip.

The group will need to allocate roles as in Activity 1 and, in this case, will need a central co-ordinator or leader to oversee the arrangements. Not only will the children be involved in putting forward their own views and ideas at the planning stage, but they will also have to carry out a practical activity which will test the planning and may call for some rearrangements. The implementation of any plans call for giving instructions, asking for and checking details, listening to comments and information and, above all, a constant review of progress towards the goal.

A review discussion after the event will prove most lively and will provide the opportunity for children to make personal but constructive comments on the activity.

I've got the 10 extra chairs for the hall. What else is needed?

### Activity 3: Personal views

Discussing a personal view of a subject close to your heart is an activity which motivates many of us to great lengths. This is especially so of children but, for the purposes of this activity, they should begin to listen with attention to the views of others and try to take them into account in some cases.

Start off by thinking up a list of subjects which are very important to the children and then arrange them in pairs and let them choose a subject to discuss. The pairs situation allows each child maximum opportunity to listen and the attention of the whole audience. They should understand that when one is speaking the other must listen and then try to comment on what has been said, possibly giving his or her view of the same point.

Subjects might include the following:

What I like/dislike about myself.
What I want to be when I grow up.
Who I would be if I were not myself.
What I would change about my family/class/school.
My ideal pet/friend/place to live.
My dream holiday.

Increase the group size but keep them small to give maximum time for the children to speak as well as listen.

### Activity 4: Debate

You can introduce debate at a class level after the children have had some experience of listening to other's views in smaller group situations. As a class activity you will be able to guide the proceedings and the more formal situation will structure the opportunities for speaking, for example, the chairperson has to give permission to speak and opposing sides take turns to air their views.

Pick two or three children to speak for and against the motion but first split the class into 'for' and 'against' sides and allow a few minutes free discussion between the members of each side before you begin. This should provide the speakers with some ideas and encourage the audience to listen carefully for their ideas to come up. Pick a number of controversial issues close to the debaters' hearts:

TV is bad for you.
Graffiti brightens up the place.
School uniform is a good thing.
Batman is a coward.
Schools should have longer holidays in winter.

Do set out the rules of debate behaviour before you begin. This more formal speaking and listening situation where permission to speak is given by the chairperson will help children to observe the same conventions in informal settings.

### Copymasters

Use **copymaster 9** (What do you think?) to form part of your work on discussion of personal views in a controversial area. The children can work in pairs. They can draw themselves (head and shoulders) and make short notes of their thoughts on the picture of a vandalised play area.

Use **copymaster 10** (Holiday choice) as another opportunity for the children to discuss a topic, this time a type of holiday, and talk about personal preferences. They can draw themselves in the snapshot frames and make notes of their ideas in the bubbles.

Use **copymaster 11** (In the news) like **copymaster 9** above to provide a controversial subject for discussion in pairs or a small group. The children are shown an incident being enacted on the television news which shows a protest going on. The picture provides the only facts available and the children can discuss the possible events that led to the incident and possible outcomes.

16

# PRESENTATIONS

## Purpose

To give the children experience of taking part in a presentation.

## Activity 1: Describing what happened

After the children have taken part in a group exercise they are usually only too willing to talk about it. This activity explores the idea of making that talk a little more formal as they have to describe something that really happened to some people who were not there. There is no room for using the imagination here, they must relate the facts and their feelings about them in such a way as to be understood by other people.

The same suggestions for organising group work apply in this situation as there will need to be a working discussion in order to arrange the presentation. The group may want to appoint a chairperson straight away to help keep everyone in order as they talk over the event, share their thoughts and impressions. They may be able at this stage to review the experience and any new knowledge, weighing each other's views and coming to a consensus of opinion. However they may have very different personal views and these are obviously part of the group experience to be presented.

The value of this exercise lies in the discussion and individual children realising that their view is as valid as the next child's. Drawing together the group's impressions of the experience into a coherent statement is quite difficult and you may need to make suggestions such as, 'Would it be right to say that most of you enjoyed the trip very much, but travel sickness spoilt the journey for some?' or, 'It sounds as though you all think the model works well.' It is essential to identify the highlights of the event such as things that were seen or done as well as presenting individual impressions. All this needs to be discussed before the children begin to plan the presentation. If the children can describe the event to you alone then they have done what this activity requires. It will take a little more confidence and organisation for them to describe it to a wider audience.

As with a written presentation, the group must consider the expected audience, their age, experience and previous knowledge. A presentation about a visit to a computer laboratory may not be riveting for the reception class, but if the group can think of a way of making it interesting for them and adapt the information to this audience then they will have learned a great deal about the differences in language and experience at different ages. They may have to seek the advice of the reception teacher to help their planning.

Any event in which all the group have taken part is suitable, for example: a class trip, designing and making an obstacle course, designing and making a model or machine, a science experiment, an art and craft activity, a visit to school by a theatre workshop or showing visitors around the school.

Use **copymaster 12** (Describing what happened) to help organise the children's thoughts. The following questions are presented for them to consider:

What can I remember about the event?
What did I enjoy most?
What did I enjoy least?
What did I find most interesting?
What do I think others would like to hear about?
How did I feel before/after the event?
Would I like to do it again?

The children could ask these questions of each other within the group to help establish their thoughts and impressions, and decide what they are going to say. They may decide to let each group member give a totally personal view or they may decide to present a group impression and let different children speak about aspects of the event. A practice session will help towards building confidence and it will also help them to review the content and amend it if necessary.

In this case the type of presentation need only be a verbal description to a small audience as long as the children have simply described what happened to others. It is an initial sortie into presentations.

## Activity 2: Improvisation

Drama starts very early with role play, pretending to be someone else and elaborating on that notion by imagining things that person would do. Finger rhymes and poems with actions also help the younger child to feel involved in the action. They love to join in with the action in stories. Everyone will recognise the infant's sense of power and achievement when he helps to blow down the Little Pigs' houses and his simulated outrage when he gasps, 'And who's been eating my porridge?' with the Three Bears. To begin to develop the experience further, children need to watch drama of different kinds from live theatre, travelling drama groups, school plays and assemblies to TV, radio and

film performances. They need to know that a drama begins and ends and that roles are assumed by the actors who pretend to be the people in a story. The idea of being someone else for a short while and doing things you may not normally do is tremendously exciting.

If offers a freedom and breadth of experience. A timid child may secretly long to be bold and brassy like one of the Ugly Sisters or brave and daring like Jack of beanstalk fame.

Start to move with small steps up the wall of growing confidence and begin with short snatches of events in role play. Quite casually ask the children to 'Do that bit again. It looked really interesting!' or, introducing a small audience, 'Show Kevin what happened when that baby was snatched from its mother.' It is sometimes enough for a young child or a very timid older one to merely hold a prop to feel they have made a major contribution to the drama. It may indeed be a major step in self-confidence for that child.

Although structured play may not be a regularly used approach for children at this stage it can be employed to assist the learning in some parts of the curriculum. For example you may have a class shop as part of your Maths work on money. Apart from the hands-on money experience you could introduce a few controversial real-life shop situations in discussion and allow the children time to try them out in the shop. For example: a child is accused of shop-lifting by the owner and the police are called; a child wants some sweets and the parent refuses; a newspaper delivery person is refused payment by the shop owner; a shop assistant gives the wrong change and refuses to see he/she is wrong; a gang of rough, rowdy youths crowd into a shop and harass the shop assistant; an old person is confused and the shop assistant helps him/her; a customer returns faulty goods; tourists who speak no English need some essential supplies.

Some children may be confident enough to try and improvise or act out the probable outcomes of such scenes in front of the class, but others will gain confidence from trying them out in a more casual

situation without an audience in the 'shop'. The power of the audience will be only too apparent to the actors and it may be helpful if you were to show the children the different ways an audience can respond. It can be polite and quiet or it can become involved in the action and hiss at the villain, sigh for a sadness and cheer for a happy outcome. In fact, children usually respond almost instinctively in this manner but when the actors are only learning their first confidence, audience response can make or break them. If you can show your audience that everyone's efforts deserve attention, appreciation and encouragement, then they will have learnt an important lesson.

Motivation being a prime factor in all learning, you may find that the children will respond to subjects which are linked to their age group and culture and which consider feelings familiar to them. Give the children regular opportunities to try out improvisations in small groups, sometimes showing them to the class and sometimes working for the participants alone. They will enjoy working on scenes from books or poems they have read or making up their own scenes about things which concern them like parent problems or group rivalry. Strategies for motivating short scenes could include:

a) Creating different episodes for characters in a book, for example, *George's marvellous medicine*, where George meets two other children who have made something marvellous.

b) Creating alternative endings to well-known stories, for example, *Cinderella*, where the Prince decides he does not like Cinderella after all.

c) Considering traditional roles from a different viewpoint, for example, *Jack and the beanstalk* where Jack was a thief, or *Goldilocks*, where she was destitute.

d) A new perspective on history, for example: pretending to be the inventor of the television explaining how it works to his friends; a person in the crowd at the running of the first locomotive, when a man was killed; a caveman describing a woolly mammoth to his friends.

e) Real-life situations the children may find themselves in or may have seen: a minor car crash, driver explaining to police/wife/husband what happened; a customer dealing with a lethargic shop assistant; a bus driver dealing with a passenger who refuses to get off; a child explaining to Dad why his car has a streak of red paint on it; Dad bringing Mum an anniversary present; a boy asking a girl for a date; a child persuading parents she really needs a new …; a child inviting a new child into his/her group.

**Copymasters**

Use **copymaster 13** (Look at it another way) as a basis for discussion. The children have to work in pairs or small groups and discuss how the behaviour of each of the characters from traditional stories can be interpreted in a different way. They can make notes of their suggestions and possibly try them out. There is also room to draw two characters of their own choosing.

18

# Attainment target 1: Speaking and listening

The development of pupils' understanding of the spoken word and the capacity to express themselves effectively in a variety of speaking and listening activities, matching style and response to audience and purpose.

| Level 5 | Statements of attainment | Example |
|---|---|---|
| | Pupils should be able to: | |
| | a) give a well organised and sustained account of an event, a personal experience or an activity. | *Describe a model which has been made, indicating the reasons for the design and the choice of materials.* |
| | b) contribute to and respond constructively in discussion, including the development of ideas; advocate and justify a point of view. | *Explain the actions taken by a character in a novel; work in a group to develop a detailed plan of action; provide arguments in favour of an approach to a problem.* |
| | c) use language to convey information and ideas effectively in a straightforward situation. | *Provide an eye witness account of an event or incident; explain how a personal possession was lost, describing the item in question.* |
| | d) contribute to the planning of, and participate in, a group presentation. | *Compile a news report or a news programme for younger children; perform a story or poem by means of improvisation, making use of video, or audio recorders where appropriate.* |
| | e) recognise variations in vocabulary between different regional or social groups, and relate this knowledge where appropriate to personal experience. | *Talk about dialect vocabulary and specialist terms; discuss the vocabulary used by characters in books or on television.* |

 **Area of study 1**

# GIVING AN ACCOUNT

 C14

## Introduction
This area of study requires the children to give a verbal account of something which has happened to them alone or as a member of a group, or of something they have seen. In this case, they are to report individually to a group or to the class to give them an increasing awareness of their own independence. It can also be an opportunity for them to watch the audience as others speak and then to try to assess how effective their own use of language has been when they are in the same situation.

The Programmes of Study suggest that the children be given opportunity to 'Express and justify feelings, opinions and viewpoints,' and to 'Present their ideas, experience and understanding in a wide range of contexts, across the curriculum and with an increasing awareness of audience and purpose.' At this level the children should be working towards being able to give a well organised account of something that happened, with events in sequence and with greater attention to

detail. In some cases they will have to justify details. Most importantly they should now be able to identify their own feelings and from this start to form their own opinions and viewpoints. Expression of personal ideas takes a little more confidence than presenting facts, especially if the speaker is required to justify those opinions. Finally, they should be working towards producing a sustained narrative and this requires good concentration.

In this area of study we are working towards developing these skills. The children will need to practise these in group and class situations and then you can gradually introduce them to reporting individually. Always be prepared to go back to a small group situation if a child begins to lose confidence.

## Purpose
To give the children practice in giving a well organised, sustained account of an event, personal experience or activity.

### Activity 1: Reporting events

In this case the children are to report what happened at an event, including the sequence of events and factual details. Suitable events could include the following: a football match, sports day, an assembly or presentation, a swimming gala, a school quiz, an important visitor to school, a visit to a place of interest.

An effective strategy for helping to recall details after an event is to tell the children they should try to remember everything that happens so that they can talk about it afterwards. Be careful to find an interesting purpose for that talk so that the children are not put off the event because they are worried about the trauma of the talk. You could arrange for children to talk to others in the class who have not been involved in the event or they could record their report on audio tape or they could tell another adult. All of these situations could be fairly casual and put forward by you in a low key manner. Alternatively, let the report form part of an assembly or a mock radio programme. The important thing is to note the order of events and prompt recall with questions such as: What happened first? Did that cause anything else to happen? What happened straight after that?

### Activity 2: Making notes

Let the children practise making notes so that they get used to noticing and remembering details and the order of events. Watch videos of sports events, excerpts from pop music programmes or episodes from children's TV dramas and get the children to watch for the sequence of happenings. Use anything that will rivet their attention. You can prompt verbally as you watch and note down the sequence of happenings in single words or phrases on the board. Let them have a go at note-taking and compare the results of individuals and groups afterwards. You can make a competition of the activity and see which of two or more groups has noted the most details. You can also do this activity verbally to help develop memory.

### Activity 3: Describing an activity

The same skills are used here: concentration, retention and recall of details. In this case, the children are to describe how something was made or done. The order of events is important to achieve the end result and in case that activity is to be repeated by others. The children can describe the materials or the processes used and the reasons for using them. Give them a working formula

for this sort of description, to help them think logically. It could be: What did we make/do? What materials did we use? Why did we use them? What did we do first/second … Did we discover any problems? How did we solve them? Was the end result what we hoped for?

A good way of testing if a description is accurate is to try and follow it as a set of instructions. Let the children practise by giving instructions to others on how to complete simple tasks such as sharpening a pencil, loading the computer, playing a game.

## Activity 4: Justifying choices

Play a game to get the children used to giving a reason for any choices they have to make.

'*Would you rather …*'     Get the children to write out things they like doing. Use one piece of paper per activity. They can be things they like eating, playing with, watching, listening to and so on. Put the papers in a bucket and let children pick out three each at random. Now the children have to pick the thing they would rather do from the three options. These activities are hypothetical and do not have to be carried out in class! They can say if they do not like any of the things but must still pick the one they prefer and give the reasons for their choice. Sometimes we do have to make the best of a situation we do not particularly like. If the players do not like all the cards, they can have the choice of swapping two of the cards for others picked at random from the bucket. Play this in groups.

Discuss topics of great importance to the children and ask them to justify their opinions. For example, discuss class/school rules, bullying or homework.

## Activity 5: Personal experiences

In this activity the children have to describe something that happened to them personally. This could be their feelings about an event or their opinion of something as a result of an experience. Whatever it is, they need to describe how they felt and to try to justify this or to give reasons for an opinion. The range of experiences might include the following: a dream, a birthday, the birth of a sibling, a sad experience, a happy experience, an awful experience or a proud time.

Use **copymaster 14** (My feelings) to give the children some experience of cataloguing their feelings on various subjects. The children are to draw themselves in the centre and fill in the bubbles with notes about their feelings. Questions include:

'I am sad if …'
'Today I feel …'
'I am good at …'

## Activity 6: Reviewing your own performance

Try to get the children into the habit of looking critically at their own performance and that of others. A good starting point is for them to ask themselves: 'Did I say what I wanted to?' 'Did they understand what I was talking about?' 'Did I miss anything out?' 'What else could I have included?' and, most importantly, 'What did I do well?' 'What did I enjoy most?'

The children need a certain amount of confidence to do this and it can only be built up over time with patience and encouragement from you as the teacher. The children need to feel confident in your help and encouragement, confident in the understanding of their classmates and confident in their own ability. They also need to have an interest in the subject and a desire to succeed. You could try getting the children into friendship pairs and ask them to review each other's performance in a positive and helpful manner and this in itself is a kind of description with which this area of study is concerned.

# MEANINGFUL DISCUSSION

**Purpose**

To encourage the children to contribute to and respond constructively in discussion, including the development of ideas; also to advocate and justify a point of view.

**Activity 1: Participating in discussion**

At this level of development the children should be encouraged to continue to read a wide variety of books. Their choice of fiction will be as varied as their general interests, and they will have definite preferences. For a group discussion it will be necessary to choose a book for this purpose and the choice may well have to be arrived at by consensus. When a book or novel has been chosen the children should be encouraged to read it. It may not be necessary to read the entire book but merely chosen sections. The discussion can then be centred upon the actions of the main character or one of the supporting characters. An alternative approach may be to read out a section of the book yourself and then invite discussion as to the reasons for a particular type of behaviour. The children can then offer their own suggestions based upon the information they obtain from the passage as it is read. An important part of the discussion is for the children to ask questions in order to clarify certain points as they arise. The answers to these questions will help to give a better picture of the situation that the character is in and the circumstances surrounding them. After the discussion a summary of all the points raised and the conclusions arrived at should be compared with the actual account in the story. This can lead to a further discussion as to how the two accounts differed or were the same. The main advantage of this is that it should encourage the children to want to find out how the character develops by reading the book for themselves.

**Activity 2: Developing a plan of action**

Children should be involved in the planning of activities and this involvement can often lead to lively debate and discussion. The range of events and activities is endless and can be as simple as arranging to swap furniture around in the classroom or as complicated as organising the school sports day. Once the activity has been chosen, a leader or co-ordinator will need to be chosen. They will have the task of deciding what needs to be done and who will do it. Obviously they cannot do everything themselves and so they need to co-opt others. The children can sort themselves into groups and each group can have a different task to plan and organise. Depending upon their task they will need to think about different things.

As an example we will take the school sports day. They will need to think about such things as the date it will take place. What happens if it is raining on that day? Will there be an alternative date? Where will the event take place? What time will it start? If parents are invited, how will they get to know the details? Are there to be arrangements for seating? Are there to be any refreshments? If so, who is going to provide them and what sort should they be? Where should the refreshment area be sited? Are the children to be allowed to buy them too? Is any special equipment needed such as loudspeakers, stop-watches, ropes or obstacles for the various races? Are any prizes to be given and, if so, what will they be? Is there to be a presentation of prizes to individuals? If so, by whom? Also, is there to be a team prize and how will the points be allocated? All these points and more can be raised and discussed. Then the allocation of tasks, the gathering of materials and the organisation of them will follow. Throughout all the discussion the children will need guidance and encouragement through careful questioning and the important thing to remember is to know when to interfere and when to leave them to themselves. The final assessment of the plan of action will also lead to further suggestions as to how it might be improved.

**Activity 3: Points of view**

Points of view vary enormously from one individual to the next. Several people viewing an event or observing the behaviour of others, respond in a variety of ways to what they see. The observation of this behaviour can be by way of a video and the children can then have the opportunity to discuss what they have seen. The video can show whatever you wish – a small playlet performed by the children and recorded by the school video camera is a good way of involving them and gives added interest. Also the subject matter can be created to suit the needs of the group and thus promote discussion. The children can be asked to justify the actions of a chosen character or say why they should not have behaved in a particular way. The rest of the group can be given the opportunity to disagree, again justifying their own points of view in the process. This activity can be further extended to include the development of ideas in other aspects of the curriculum.

In CDT, for example, the discussion of the design brief can lead to an expression of strong points of view regarding the use and type of materials, the method of construction and the mode of operation. This in turn will lead to a development of ideas as the various aspects of the design evolve. The same design brief can be given to several different groups of children and they each have to come up with ideas to solve the problem. They work independently and come up with their own solutions. Then the groups come together and compare and discuss their solutions, providing arguments for their own ideas, justifying them and, if they disagree strongly about any aspect of the solutions offered by one of the other groups, to argue against them and be prepared to justify their opposition.

# LANGUAGE FOR INFORMATION

C15 –16

## Purpose

To encourage the children to use language to convey information and ideas effectively in a straightforward situation.

## Activity 1: Eyewitness report

Using events or activities which take place in or around school, the children can try to give their own eyewitness reports. If the event can be recorded in some way, either with a video camera, an ordinary camera or a tape recorder, then this will give an opportunity to review their report and assess the level of accuracy. The BBC television programme *Crimewatch* often stages reconstructions of crimes and, provided care is taken over the choice of subject, one of the less sensational topics could be used to develop the children's powers of observation. After viewing it without the commentary one of the children could be asked to give an eyewitness account of the events including detailed descriptions of characters, places and vehicles involved. A review of the recording can help to highlight any discrepancies after the initial account.

## Activity 2: Description of personal possessions

Many people can be in possession of a personal item and never really take the time to look at it properly. A useful exercise is to encourage the children to think about a personal item such as a watch, a piece of jewellery or any item of clothing that they happen to be wearing at the time and ask them to describe it in detail without looking at it. If the item is a piece of jewellery, try to obtain it from the child before they start their description. You could conceal it behind a small screen so that you can observe the item as the description is being given. Also, if necessary, you can help them in their description by asking questions about what the item is made of. How big is it? Does it have any distinguishing features such as colour, design, shape, unusual safety fastener or the fact that it performs a particular function. The activity can be extended by asking the children to imagine that they have lost the particular item and they have to give a detailed account as to how it was lost. Was the loss a result of carelessness, because they left it behind somewhere, or did the safety catch break and the item fall to the ground without them noticing it? Encourage as wide a variety of reasons as possible from the children.

## Copymasters

Use **copymaster 15** (Eyewitness report) for the children to write down in as much detail as possible one of the items from a video of a national news broadcast. The item should be watched in silence. Afterwards they can record their immediate response on an audio tape recorder. Then they can watch the video again and write down their observations as they watch. The two accounts can then be compared and checked to see how well they were able to recall the details.

Use **copymaster 16** (Lost and found) to write a description of a lost item saying where and how it was lost, for inclusion in the lost and found column of a local newspaper. Encourage the children to give as much detail as they can in the briefest possible way.

# GROUP PRESENTATIONS

C17

## Purpose

To give the children practice in planning and participating in a group presentation.

## Materials needed

Card, pens, scissors, an assortment of props, video recorder and tape recorder.

## Activity 1: Planning

See p. 17 where describing the outcome of a group activity is dealt with as a presentation. At this level the children should be working towards planning such presentations in a group situation with minimum intervention from you. Get them into the habit of working with guidelines such as the following:

- organise roles in the group (chairperson, notetaker etc.)
- note: subject, audience, length of time available
- decide on form of presentation

- write or plan presentation
- allocate roles (speaking, stage managing)
- list and organise any props
- start rehearsals.

## Activity 2: Presenting the news

The first things to decide are:

- the type of presentation (quick report, feature programme)
- the age of the audience (peers or younger children)
- what area of news to present (class, school, local or world news or a mixture)
- what items to include (personal interest, politics, accidents, crime, sport, weather, entertainment, fashion)
- how long the programme will be
- the form of presentation (live or recorded on audio or video tape).

23

The news is a short factual programme presented in the form of a report. It needs to present a lot of material in a short time as quickly and clearly as possible. The children should take this into account when planning the content of the programme. They may need to do some initial investigative journalism to gather material and then meet as a group to decide which items are suitable for the programme, how long each item should be and what order they are going to present them in. They will also have to be aware that their 'facts' will need to be checked carefully. They will need to decide whether to alternate good news with bad and whether or not it is a good idea to finish on the positive note of a lighthearted item.

If the children decide to record the presentation, either in audio or video form, this will give them the added advantage of being able to edit parts they decide are unsuitable and to re-take any parts which they feel are not good enough for whatever reason. The whole programme can be recorded or special items can be highlighted with a recorded audio interview with the man/woman of the moment, video footage of the scene of interest or, indeed, an outside broadcast.

In the case of recorded presentations the groups will need some members to have mainly technical roles, but

for the purposes of this attainment target you will need to ensure that each child has some experience of the speaking roles too.

**Activity 3: Improvising stories or poems**
At this level the children should be working towards planning and presenting complete performances of an imaginative nature. These can be in the form of improvisations of published stories or poems or those written by themselves. This area of study is concerned with the children inventing their own dialogue around a plot and getting so immersed in a role that they even change the dialogue from one performance to the next, while keeping the story line and characterisation intact. There is no set script, but if the children lack confidence initially, they can draft out a script as a general guideline but allow themselves to change the lines when they perform them. This really stretches the imagination, the memory and the understanding of the characterisation and plot.

Again, group work is the key approach. See pp. 17–18 for ideas for improvisations of the pupil's own devising. The children will need to co-operate sympathetically and prompt each other if 'words fail'. This sort of activity is very useful for development of reasoning and imagination. The children will need to talk about the characters portrayed in the story or poem and decide from that information what they would say and how they would speak and behave in the given situation. This can be great fun as children often throw themselves into a role with refreshing spontaneity.

**Copymasters**
Use **copymaster 17** (Programme planner) to help the children in the initial stages of planning a presentation or programme. They can make their own notes under the headings: Programme subject, order of items, presenters etc.

# DIALECTS

## Purpose
To encourage recognition of variations in vocabulary between different regional or social groups.

## Activity 1: Looking at regional variations in vocabulary
Due to social and geographical mobility it is more than likely that most classrooms will have children from a variety of backgrounds. These days many families have had to move to a completely different area of the country when the family has had to move because of employment.

So children will probably have experience of vocabulary differences from their own friends. If there are any children in the class who have moved to the area from a long distance encourage them to talk about the differences they have noticed. Are they used to calling familiar objects by different names where they came from? The children can be set a task to find as many different regional words for the same objects as they can. Terms of friendship or endearment can also be a good source of variation regionally and the children will have fun trying to be the one to discover the most expressions. Children from different ethnic backgrounds will also have a rich variety of phrases and sayings which will also help to highlight these differences. Try to compile a tape recording of different regional accents and vocabulary. The accents can often give strong clues as to the location of the language and the children can at first be asked to try and recognise from where the accent comes.

Try them first with Scottish, Irish, English and Welsh dialects. Then make it a little more difficult with dialects from cities like Birmingham, Liverpool, Newcastle and Glasgow. Often the understanding of vocabulary is hindered by dialect so the children will need to become accustomed to this. The next step is to try and understand what is being said by listening carefully to the context in which it is spoken. It must be said that listening carefully is the most important aspect in the development of the appreciation of these variations of vocabulary and clues as to the meaning of unfamiliar words or phrases can be obtained by listening to the entire sentence. The children can be encouraged to keep a dialect vocabulary so that they can look for similarities and differences in words with the same meaning from different regions of the country.

## Activity 2: Variations between social groups
When we talk about social groups many people immediately think in terms of the working-, middle- and upper-class socio-economic groups. Belonging to one of these groups is often associated with the type of house we live in, where we live, the sort of job we do or even the type of car we drive. Alongside all these so-called indicators is vocabulary. The way we speak is supposed to give a good indication of social background. Many people learn to disguise 'humble' beginnings and talk posh. As a result it is not quite so easy to categorise people as it was at the turn of the century. People tend to talk in the way that makes them acceptable to their friends and the people they work with. A person who uses long complicated words on the shop floor might be very much out of place and would probably embarrass his co-workers or be subjected to ridicule as they try to come to terms with his strange vocabulary. Similarly children have their own acceptable phrases which they use to show that they want to be just like the rest of their group.

Discuss this with the children and ask what sort of vocabulary they would find unacceptable from a member of their class. Would it be just the vocabulary or might it be something to do with the way it is spoken? Ask them to try to compare similar phrases and try to show how different social groups might construct them. An example might be: 'Would you like to come to the cinema with me?' compared with: 'What about comin' to the pictures eh?'

The children can have fun trying to think of such phrases and comparing them. Split the class into two groups and let one group give their phrase while the other group translates it.

Regional television companies produce such programmes as *Coronation Street*, *Brookside*, *Emmerdale Farm*, and the vocabulary can be contrasted with other such programmes as *Take the High Road*, *EastEnders* and *Only Fools and Horses*. The children can watch parts of episodes and see whether they can understand the language or if there are any parts they find difficult. They can also be encouraged to look at local poetry from different parts of the country.

25

# ATTAINMENT TARGET 2: Reading

## Attainment target 2: Reading

The development of the ability to read, understand and respond to all types of writing, as well as the development of information-retrieval strategies for the purposes of study.

| Level 3 | Statements of attainment | Example |
|---|---|---|
| | Pupils should be able to: | |
| | a) read aloud from familiar stories and poems fluently and with appropriate expression. | *Raise or lower voice to indicate different characters.* |
| | b) read silently and with sustained concentration. | |
| | c) listen attentively to stories, talk about setting, story-line and characters and recall significant details. | *Talk about a story, saying what happened to change the fortunes of the leading characters.* |
| | d) demonstrate, in talking about stories and poems, that they are beginning to use inference, deduction and previous reading experience to find and appreciate meanings beyond the literal. | *Discuss what might happen to characters in a story, based on the outcome of adventures in other stories.* |
| | e) bring to their writing and discussion about stories some understanding of the way stories are structured. | *Refer to different parts of the story such as 'at the beginning' or 'the story ends with'; notice that some stories build up in a predictable way, eg. 'The Three Little Pigs', 'Goldilocks and the Three Bears'.* |
| | f) devise a clear set of questions that will enable them to select and use appropriate books from the class and school library. | *Decide that the wildlife project needs information about the size and colour of birds, their food and habitat, and look it up.* |

 Area of study 1

## READING ALOUD

 C18

**Purpose**
To give children practice in reading aloud with appropriate expression.

**Activity 1: Reading aloud**
In order to read aloud with appropriate expression the reader must be able to understand the text so that he or she knows the type of character who is speaking and also knows something about how to portray feelings or expressions by using different tones of voice. These changes of tone are also important in setting the mood

or atmosphere of the text. Even before a child can read fluently he or she can be made aware of the importance of tone of voice as an indicator of mood by listening to an adult reading favourite stories. The many tapes available commercially are also very useful for this purpose. Whatever the story the tone of the voice and the way the story is read will help to make it much more meaningful. Important points such as pausing at dramatic points, speeding up or slowing down to suit the pace of the action, raising and lowering the voice to dramatise events or speech will all give the children good examples of how a story ought to be read. Reading the story fairly slowly and enunciating carefully should ensure that they do not miss any of the text, and the children should be involved where possible in the story by being asked to speak just like one of the characters.

Children are usually very good at imitating voices they have heard on television or radio, and also of people they know. They should come to realise that certain characters always have a similar kind of voice, for example, a witch's cackle or the metallic monotone of a robot. At the same time they should be developing the confidence to use their repertoire of voices when they read out loud for themselves. Fluency in reading comes from knowledge, practice and self confidence, so children need lots of practice and opportunities to read out loud to you, a small group of peers or younger children and sometimes to larger groups such as the class or in an assembly. At every opportunity let them read out loud what they have written, let them read out to the rest of the class their favourite poem or nursery rhyme, encourage them to read stories to younger members of a different class and always encourage them to develop a range of different voices for different reading purposes.

## Activity 2: Developing a repertoire of voices

Puppets are very useful in developing a wide range of different voices among children. This activity will be more meaningful if the children have the opportunity to make their own character puppet and then devise a simple puppet show which gives them the chance to portray that character. Shy or reticent children will often express themselves far better through a puppet, than standing up in front of the rest of the children to read from a text. They can immerse themselves in the character and, if the puppet play is performed in a little puppet theatre, they can hide behind the screen if they so wish. This activity helps them to build confidence in the portrayal of a character through the use of a different voice. The watching group can be encouraged to offer constructive comments after seeing the puppet play and by exchanging the puppets between themselves for different performances they can observe similarities and differences in people's interpretation of how the character should be portrayed. The activity can be extended by asking the children to place the character in an unfamiliar situation or by having such things as a good witch or a gentle giant, and encouraging the children to show this by the way the character speaks.

## Activity 3: Raising and lowering the voice to indicate character

Different characters will obviously have different voices and the children can have lots of fun experimenting with set phrases to try and convey what type of character is speaking. They can work in groups and take it in turn to read or say a line of dialogue and the rest of the group have to try to identify the age of the character, whether it is male or female, whether it is good or bad, big or little, happy or sad.

## Copymasters

Use **copymaster 18** (Talking heads) as an exercise in matching a suitable voice to one of the pictures. The children are to work in a small group, and one can be the leader. Each child should have a copy of the sheet and the leader chooses one child and indicates which character the child has to interpret. The child then has to read or make up a simple phrase in the way they think the character would speak. The activity can be extended by asking the children to show an emotion at the same time. They might, for example, be asked to speak like an old person who is sad.

27

# SILENT READING

## Purpose
To provide encouragement for silent reading and sustained concentration.

## Materials needed
A good supply of books, a quiet place, soft furnishings, tapes and tape recorders with headphones.

## Activity 1: A reading corner
Cosy reading corners are a feature of many infant schools and there is no doubt that careful attention to such details does contribute to the effectiveness of the reading environment. These details are just as important as the children get older.

Try to ensure that there is somewhere in each classroom which is set aside for a quiet corner to give the children the opportunity to sit quietly and reflect, read or listen to audio tapes with headphones. The main school library also needs a quiet venue, if possible.

Make this place as comfortable as possible with a piece of carpet, large cushions or comfy chairs and colourful posters. Display the books carefully so that they look inviting and the covers are visible. You may also wish to highlight new books, books on a particular topic or to bring books to notice that have not been used for a while.

## Activity 2: Creating a purpose
Make a definite allocation of time for the purpose of silent reading when the children know that for a specified time they can read to themselves. You can organise this for groups or the whole class on a regular basis. Peer coercion can often make a task attractive! Having said that, by this stage readers are often very happy to be given a period of relative relaxation to enjoy books. To this end do not allocate a specific task or quiz the children about what they have read afterwards. However you can try to develop a sort of community spirit about the enterprise so that the children casually share impressions of what has been read, pass on a good book to a friend and enjoy the activity for its own sake. Try to give it a priority status by your own positive attitude and by encouraging a sense of anticipation in the children as the time draws near. The purpose of the activity is to encourage concentration, commitment and enjoyment of reading.

## Activity 3: Listening and reading
There are now many books which have an accompanying audio tape which provides an exact match of words and a page turner cue. Many good examples of popular children's literature are produced on audio tape at reasonable prices. Although not a strictly silent reading activity, listening to a tape and following the words is a great aid to concentration because it is absorbing and enjoyable, like a combination of storytelling and reading at the same time.

## Activity 4: Ensuring a good supply of books
Try to keep a selection of fiction and nonfiction in your book corner. Some schools have individual class library supplies and others have a central source and allow each classroom to change its supply on a regular basis. Your local library service may have a school loans section for fiction and nonfiction. Whatever the supply source try to stock up with books that will appeal to the children. Try to involve the children in the selection and find out about current interests. Of course, the children in any one class are interested in a range of topics and types of literature, so try to include as much variety as possible, both in content and style of presentation.

It is important to make all the books available to all of the children. It is our task to stimulate interest, broaden horizons and make all children feel good about books and reading.

## Activity 5: Literary criticism
Occasionally you can supply a reason for silent reading and at the same time stimulate the children's interest and critical facility. If you have an influx of new books or a new supply from the central source, make this into an opportunity to try a little literary criticism. Do not make the task too daunting. You can ask the children to place in order of preference several books on the same topic or several different versions of the same story, or simply a small selection of new titles.

## Copymasters
Use **copymaster 19** (Book of the month) for this activity. The children can use the space to put three books in order of preference and give brief reasons for the decision. Have a 'Book of the month'!

Use **copymaster 20** (Book report) to record greater detail about single books. A ring binder can be used to collect the sheets.

# STORY-LINE AND DETAILS

## Introduction

The prerequisite for this area of study is reading experience. The children need to have read or heard a great variety of stories, from traditional tales to modern authors such as Roald Dahl, C. S. Lewis, Shirley Hughes etc. TV programmes often have 'the book of the series' and indeed stories are read on TV as well as being dramatised. There are many series for children in which the main set of characters have different adventures. Encourage the children to bring in their favourite books to show classmates. You could set aside a special time to do this when you can all talk about the books in a casual way, sharing impressions. A love of reading is important if the children are to attempt to analyse stories. Concentration needs continuous development and this can be encouraged by reading stories which the children enjoy, that are well written and grip the attention. Stories split into chapters or episodes are good for maintaining interest. Allocate a special time for listening to stories, daily if possible. Make time for silent reading as part of this experience. See p. 28.

## Purpose

To give the children practice in recognising settings, story-lines, characters and significant details in the plot of stories.

## Materials needed

A selection of good books, videos and comics.

## Activity 1: Sharing views and getting down to the basics of story analysis

Get into the habit of talking about stories which have been read in class, heard on TV or radio, or seen as a TV drama series. Share views about the characters and the plots, talking about what the characters look like, their personalities and what they do in the stories. Encourage the children to give their own opinions of the characters' behaviour in the story plot, but always try to get them to give some evidence of this from the actual story. Discuss the setting of the stories, where the action took place, whether there was more than one place and how important this was to the story. (In the real life account of Scott's expedition to the Antarctic the setting was all important in the drama.)

Discuss the story-line: is it funny, serious, scary or exciting? Do the fortunes of the characters change during the story and, if so, when does this happen? Is there a significant event which causes this change or turning point?

## Activity 2: Finding significant details and turning points

In *Charlie and the Chocolate factory*, by Roald Dahl, Charlie's fortune changes when he finds the last golden ticket! Children need to be helped to identify significant details and turning points in stories. One significant detail everyone knows is the finding of the glass slipper in *Cinderella*. It is only by careful reading and listening, highlighting examples and by much discussion that the children will begin to appreciate the importance of such points.

Make an exercise of this to help the children to recognise these details. Find a selection of well-known stories and discuss them to find the turning points and significant details and note them down. You can make a poster which will show this and act as an *aide-mémoire* for the children. Practice will greatly help this analytical skill.

Use a storyboard to aid discussion. This can be drawn on the board or **copymaster 21** can be used by children working in pairs or small groups. They can also use it to make their own notes from yours on the board.

| Have you spotted these details? | | |
|---|---|---|
| | significant details | turning points |
| Cinderella | | F.G.M. appears. Prince finds slipper. |
| The Witches | | Mouse escapes. |
| Jack and the Beanstalk | | Jack is gullible when he meets dwarf. Mother angry about beans. |
| Paddington Bear | Speaks Marma | He meets the Browns. |

**Activity 4: Drawing from experience**

Using examples from the children's own reading experience, think of several very different settings, characters and main events from stories. You can note them on the board as you all talk. Then split into groups and ask the children to make up a story using any combination of the different components. They can tell their story to the rest of the class, draw a picture to illustrate it, or they can produce a sequence of pictures to show the story.

**Copymasters**

Use **copymaster 21** (Storyboard). The story-line can also be represented diagrammatically for discussion purposes. Comic strips are basically illustrated story-lines, although some are more explicit in detailing the sequence of events than others. Collect a few examples of comic stories to look at and highlight the sequential nature of events. You can ask the children to do their own illustrated story strips but help them at first by giving them a selection of well-known short stories which have a clear sequence of events without any subplots. For example, *Goldilocks and the Three Bears*, *Brer Rabbit and the Tar Baby* and *Red Riding Hood*.

You can also use a story map. This can be in diagrammatic or note form and basically shows who the main characters are, the setting, the main events and the ending. At this level it is advisable to keep it simple and use it as a basis for discussion. For more able children use copymaster 22.

Use **copymaster 22** (How is the story made?) to help you analyse a story or to use as an assessment sheet. You have to read to the children a story that they are not familiar with or have never heard. They have to try to identify the setting, main characters, story-line and, if possible, significant details and turning points. This can be done in pairs or small groups and can be written or verbal. The sheet can be enlarged to use as a guide for discussion in Activity 2.

Use **copymaster 23** (Main events) to give the children practice in identification of the main events and a chance to invent some. The sheet shows a beginning and an ending for a story and the children have to think of and either draw or write notes of what an appropriate main event might be.

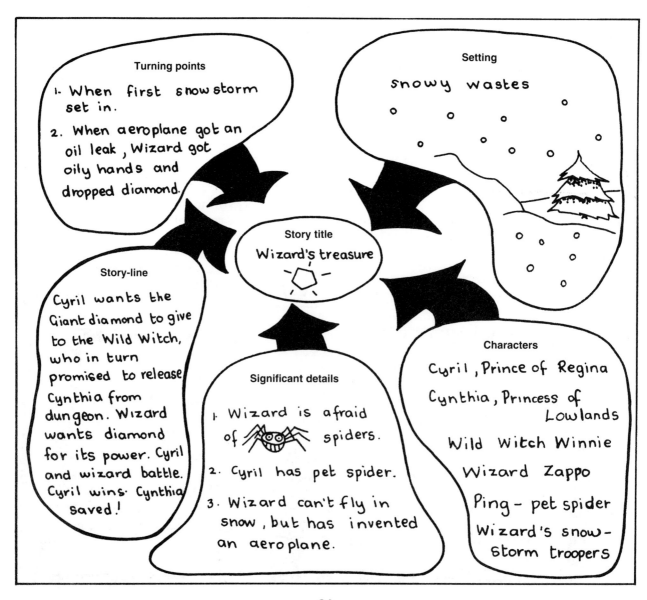

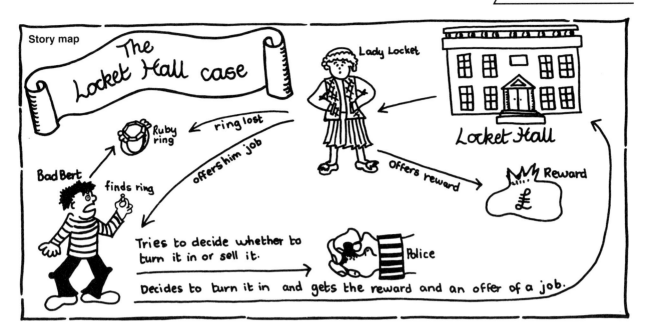

C24 –26

| Area of study 4 | **CHARACTERS IN STORIES** | |

## Purpose

To give the children a wide experience of stories with similar characters, and to encourage them to discuss possible outcomes of an adventure, based upon previous reading experience.

## Materials needed

A selection of different stories with similar characters, and a selection of different stories about the same character or set of characters.

## Activity 1: Talking about favourite characters

Conduct a simple survey among the children in your class to identify their favourite characters.

Use **copymaster 24** (Favourite character) to analyse what it is about the character they particularly like.

Fill in the details like this:

Once the information has been collected discuss the results with the children and try to establish the most popular character and the reasons why. The next step is to collect several stories featuring this character and try to see if there are any similarities in the way that the stories develop. Are the situations similar? Does the character behave in a similar or predictable way in each story? Are the stories always set in the same location with a familiar set of supporting characters? Maybe the character has an important job to do, or maybe he or she always makes a mess of things. Do all the stories have a happy ending? Discuss all these questions and you will help the children to identify any patterns of plot related to a set of books or character and this in turn will help them to predict the outcome of stories. Then, by drawing upon previous reading experience, they should be able to make a more informed prediction as to how the character will behave or the possible conclusion of the story.

**Activity 2: Comparing different characters who behave in a similar way**

Once you have looked in detail at the exploits of one character, it should then be possible to compare them with those of a different but similar one. Try to find two different series of books which contain one major character and look for all the things that are similar.

Use **copymaster 25** (Comparing characters). The children should start off by writing in the space at the top of the sheet the name of the character and the title of the book from which it comes. They can then draw a picture to illustrate the character and tick off in the boxes at the side those characteristics which apply. The space in the boxes below can be used either to draw a picture or to make short notes relevant to the heading of each box. The space at the bottom is for any other important information which might be useful. By filling in several of these sheets the children can compile a folder of characters for comparison. These can include monsters, giants, witches, wizards, pirates, aliens, dragons, kings and queens, and any other heroes and villains.

**Activity 3: Invent a story about a favourite character**

Allow the children to choose their favourite character, then ask them to try and invent a really strange situation for the character to be in. Initially this could be done as a group discussion but there would have to be agreement on choice of character. Once this is agreed each child can be given the chance to suggest an unusual situation. There is no limit to the suggestions and it is quite acceptable that a character such as King Arthur, for example, should meet aliens from outer space. As a follow up the children can be encouraged to write their own stories. Another approach could be to give the children a variety of different settings and ask them to suggest from their previous reading experience a character that would best fit into that setting and then try to create an adventure. Again this can be introduced as a group activity and, once the children have grasped the idea, they can attempt to create their own stories.

**Copymasters**

Use **copymaster 26** (Crystal gazing) to predict how one well-known character might behave in a particular situation. Their suggestions and ideas should be based upon previous reading experience of the character and their behaviour and actions in the story should reflect this. This copymaster uses the characters of Robin Hood and Maid Marian. The children can choose what kind of situation Robin and Marian find themselves in and decide how they resolve it. The children can use the copymaster to make notes if they are to give an oral presentation to a selected audience or, if they prefer, use it as the first sheet when writing their own adventure story.

As an extension the picture of Robin and Marian can be blocked out by covering it with a piece of paper before photocopying. The resulting blank space on the photocopy can then be used for the children to draw their own picture or another illustration can be glued on for the children to write about.

| Area of study 5 | **STORY STRUCTURE** |  C27 −29 |

**Purpose**

To give the children further experience of simple story analysis. (The children need as much experience as possible of a variety of stories delivered in several ways. Try to give the children different reading and listening situations, sometimes alone, in pairs, small groups or as a class.)

**Materials needed**

A variety of stories, listening tapes and video stories.

**Activity 1: Discovery discussions**

Start off by discussing very well-known stories which are fairly short and have a well defined story-line which builds up in a predictable way. Stories such as *The Three Little Pigs*, *Rumpelstiltskin* and *Goldilocks and the Three Bears* are useful even at this level as the

children will enjoy the trip back to younger days. You can also use modern classics such as stories about Paddington Bear, Popeye, Super Ted and *Charlotte's Web*.

When you discuss the stories afterwards, refer to different parts of the story as the 'beginning, middle and end'. Talk about the children's preferences for different events or characters in the stories and see if they can tell you when events took place. 'Did your favourite exciting bit happen at the very beginning or at the end?' (If the answer is 'no', then it must have been in the middle!)

It is fairly easy to identify the beginning and ending of a story, but children do need to realise that there is a sequence of events. Try to organise your discussions as a kind of discovery process with you as the one who does not quite understand and ask for the children's help with questions such as, 'Did Jack get the golden harp

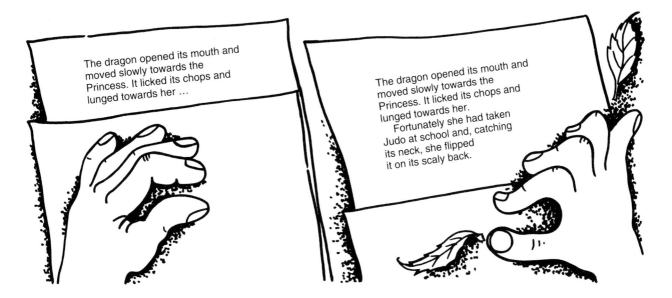

before he got the gold or was it afterwards, I can't remember?' so that attention is focused on the sequence of events.

The first turning point usually heralds the middle of the story featuring the main event or events and so marks the end of the 'beginning'. Try to get the children to recognise when this happens by asking questions such as: What was everything like at the beginning? Did anything happen to change this? How did things change? What happened next?

Discuss cause and effect by linking the final outcome of events with the situation at the beginning and by so doing you will be further emphasising the different sections of story. See pp. 30–1 for story maps and sequential story-line strips.

### Activity 2: Quiz time

Organise quiz games to test recall of events in the sequence of well-known stories. The class can be split into two halves or small teams, or you can play 'Master Mind', having one player on the spot at a time. Watch a story video, listen to a story, read or listen to a story tape and then have a selection of questions ready that will prompt the children to recall details about the story's sequential structure: 'For one point, did Paddington meet the Browns at the station or later on?' 'For two points, what was the last thing that happened to Cinderella, in the story?'

### Activity 3: Mix and match

Work in small groups and give the children a selection of about six short stories to read which can each be read in about one minute. There should be enough for them to be able to swap stories and read through most of the selection.

The children now have to work together to select a beginning, middle, an ending and a set of characters they most like from the set of stories and make a new story from these components. For example, Rupert Bear may start off at Paddington Station, get on a train to the seaside by accident and fall off the quayside into the mouth of Monstro the whale (from *Pinocchio*). They are in effect using the structural components of other stories to construct one of their own. The idea is to gather ideas for stories from different books and so learn about story structure through this process of analysis and synthesis.

This can be a purely oral exercise or the children can use a storyboard or story map (see **copymasters 22** and **28**) to record the details in note form.

### Activity 4: Prediction

Read the beginning of a story to the children and then ask them to give suggestions for what could happen next. You can then go on to read the next part of the story where a main event occurs, stop at a gripping point and ask them to try to predict the next event, based on what they have heard. Carry on and see if the children can guess the ending. This is an excellent exercise for encouraging the children to think ahead and to recall details they have heard to form the basis of their prediction.

### Copymasters

Use **copymaster 27** (What happens next?) to give further practice in prediction. The children have to read the beginning of the story and then draw what they think might be the main event of the story. They can think about the ending and possibly write this out as a separate exercise.

Use **copymaster 28** (My own story) with the three sections for the children to either draw or write the beginning, middle and the end or use a combination of both, drawing the beginning and end and writing the middle part.

Use **copymaster 29** (My favourite part) as an exercise to highlight the separate sections of a story. You will need to read the story *Charlotte's Web* to the children and then ask them to think carefully about which was their favourite part of the story. It may be the beginning, one of the main events or the ending. They have to draw this and then write down one or two reasons for their choice.

# USING THE LIBRARY

**Purpose**
To discuss and devise with the children a set of questions which will enable them to find information from the class and school library.

**Materials**
A selection of suitable reference books with contents and index lists, a set of children's encyclopedias.

**Activity 1: Devising a set of questions**
When starting on a topic discuss with the children the sort of questions they will need to ask themselves in order to find out as much as possible about their topic. First of all help them to decide whether the topic comes under one of the broad headings of an area of the curriculum such as History, Geography or Science or whether it contains elements of some or all of these. This will help the children when they start looking for relevant books in the class or school library. Give the children a supply of books on many subjects and ask them to sort them into broad subject categories simply by looking at the covers. Extend this by then asking the children to select from the pile of books all those which they think might be useful in helping them to find information about, for example, water. When they have selected those books, ask them to look through them again and make a second selection of those they would like to use based upon the readability of the text and the suitability of the illustrations.

Once the topic has been chosen the children will need to think about the aspects of the topic they wish to find out about in detail. As a group exercise discuss the aspects which should and could be included in the topic. The children can, as a group, offer suggestions and you could act as scribe to produce a topic web. This might look something like the one shown below.

Give the children plenty of practice in planning several topic webs in this way by supplying books on many different subjects and asking them to pick out which areas of study they would like to pursue. Give them the opportunity to discuss them among themselves and with you, in order to fill any gaps or to limit the depth of study. Once the areas for study have been decided the children will then need to know how to go about finding the information in books.

**Activity 2: Using a contents list**
Most information books have a table of contents near the beginning of the book. This can be used as a guide when information is needed about a particular aspect of the subject of the book, and it helps to save time searching through the pages of the book for the relevant information.

Use **copymaster 30** (Table of contents) to give the children practice in finding the right pages for the information they need. The children are to look at the contents list, and using a separate sheet of paper for the answers, write the name of the section, with the page

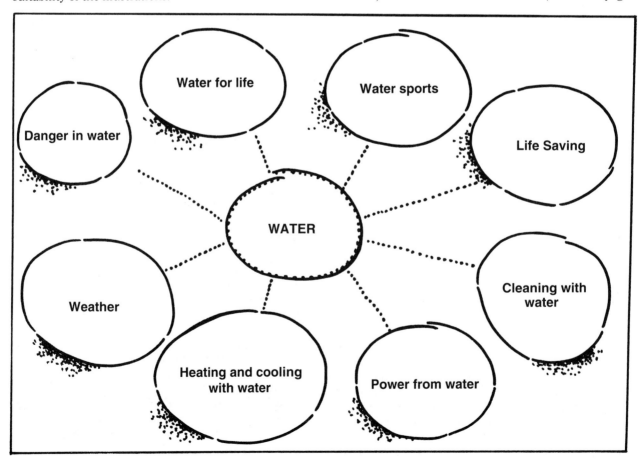

34

number on which it begins, where they would be most likely to find the answer to each question on the copymaster.

You can give further practice in the use of a contents list by devising your own set of simple questions based upon the contents lists of a variety of chosen books. There should be a series of questions for each book and, once the children have had lots of practice in this, they can work in groups to devise their own set of questions for their chosen book and these can then be interchanged between groups to give further practice in the use of a table of contents.

### Activity 3: Using the index

The index is found at the back of the book. This is a much more detailed breakdown of what can be found in the book, and instead of simply stating the page where a particular aspect of the subject of the book begins, it lists each page in the book where information about that aspect may be found.

Use **copymaster 31** (Index list) to give the children practice in looking at the way in which a topic can be broken down into many sub-headings. This can also be of help to the children when they are at the planning stage, since it may give them an idea of which areas to look at. Part of the index of a book about water is reproduced on the copymaster. Give the children practice in finding various sections by asking them to look quickly down the list to find the section on, for example, dams, then ask them to say on which pages the information will be found. Give lots of practice in this by asking for information on several different aspects of the topic. The children have to refer to the list in order to give the page number or numbers. The children can then look at the box on the right hand side of the copymaster. This asks them to write the page numbers where information may be found about those aspects of water listed. To extend this, choose books with an index list and let the children choose a topic. They can then plan the topic by creating a topic web based upon the information to be found in that book, and next to each area of study give the page reference from the index list where the relevant information may be found.

### Activity 4: Finding information in a set of encyclopedias

Many sets of encyclopedias are set out in several volumes and the spine of each book shows the letters of the alphabet for the initial letter of the subjects contained in that volume.

Use **copymaster 32** (Finding information in an encyclopedia) to give the children practice in identifying in which volume of a set of encyclopedias the information they need will be found. The illustration shows the spines of a set of encyclopedias and each spine shows the letters of the alphabet and the number of the volume. If the children want information about rockets they look along the row to see which volume has entries beginning with the letter 'R'. This is volume nine so the answer is 'Rockets–9'. The object of the copymaster is for the children to identify the volume for each of the subjects shown. They can write the correct number in

the box at the side. We have kept the initial letters simple to get the idea across but most sets of encyclopedias show two initial letters such as Ek-Fm, and practice in looking for information in a set of books like this can be undertaken using the school's own books.

### Activity 5: Where do I find the book I need?

If the books in the classroom fall short of the requirements of the children, they will need to be directed to the school library or the local library. Before they go you will need to show them how to use it. Of course they will need to be able to read the category labels if they are to find the books for themselves but, if they cannot do this, the librarian will help them. As an introduction, take the children to the school library and play a game with them, 'Hunt the book'.

Ask them to find a book about History, then ask them to find a book about nature. This will give them practice in becoming familiar with the layout of the library so that they know the position of the main subject categories. When they know this, ask for a book which contains some information about a particular aspect of a topic. This will give them practice in using their skills in reading the contents and index lists. Keep the requests simple and, as always, make the activity fun. If anyone has particular difficulty, be supportive and encourage the other children to offer advice.

### Copymasters

Use **copymaster 33** (Choosing the right book) as a way of identifying the title of the book most likely to contain the answers to the questions. The children are to look at the questions and then at the illustration on the spines of books on a book shelf. They must choose the title which they think will contain the answer they need. They can then write that title in the space provided.

Viking ships could be in this book.

# Attainment target 2: Reading

The development of the ability to read, understand and respond to all types of writing, as well as the development of information-retrieval strategies for the purposes of study.

| Level 4 | Statements of attainment | Example |
|---|---|---|
| | **Pupils should be able to:** | |
| | a) read aloud expressively, fluently and with increased confidence from a range of familiar literature. | *Vary the pace and tone of the voice to express feelings, or to represent character or mood.* |
| | b) demonstrate in talking about a range of stories and poems which they have read, an ability to explore preferences. | *Describe those qualities of the poem or story which appeal and give an indication of personal response.* |
| | c) demonstrate, in talking about stories, poems, non-fiction and other texts, that they are developing their abilities to use inference, deduction and previous reading experience. | *Recognise and use those clues in a text which help the reader predict events.* |
| | d) find books or magazines in the class or school library by using the classification system, catalogue or database and use appropriate methods of finding information, when pursuing a line of inquiry. | *Use search reading to contribute to an inquiry into health and safety at school or in the home.* |

 **Area of study 1**

# READING EXPRESSIVELY

 C34

## Purpose

To encourage the children to read aloud confidently, with expression and fluency.

## Activity 1: Using the voice to create mood, or show feelings

When the children have had lots of experience using different voices to portray character, it will be useful to direct their attention to the use of voice to create mood and atmosphere in a story. As an example of this the children could read a passage from a ghost story. Ask them what sort of voice they would use. Would it be the same sort of voice as the one they would use when reading a funny story or an exciting adventure story? Ask they how they would change their voices in order to convey a sense of mystery or excitement. Give them a short passage and ask them to read it in a variety of ways to create a different mood each time. You could give them an example by reading the account of the appearance of the ghost of Jacob Marley from *A Christmas Carol* by Charles Dickens. First of all read it in an appropriate way with a slow deliberate voice. At the same time involve the children by asking them to suggest a suitable 'ghostly' voice for the apparition. They could also suggest voices for the three Christmas ghosts. This could lead to a discussion of how the three

would speak remembering that they are three very different ghosts needing three very different voices.

To stress the importance of the use of the voice in creating mood and atmosphere, you could read the same passage in a totally unsuitable way and ask the children for their reactions and comments. Do this several times with different short texts and contrast the way each text is read. Emphasise that it is the speed of reading and the tone of voice that either creates or destroys the mood and atmosphere. Allow the children to read aloud to a variety of audiences and encourage critical reactions from the audience by asking them to try to assess the suitability of the tone and speed of the voice, and also to offer constructive advice wherever necessary.

## Activity 2: Expressing emotion

As the children become more confident in reading with expression, encourage further reading of simple texts in a variety of ways. A fun way of practising reading aloud is to take one simple text that all of them can read and ask them to read it, one at a time, and show a different emotion each time. One child might read it in a happy way, another in a very sad way. Another could show great and mounting excitement as they read it and another could read it in a very nervous or frightened way. Explore the entire range of emotions to give the children experience of them.

### Activity 3: Different character voices

Most children are familiar with the typical voices of a wicked witch, angry giant, ghost and robot, to name but a few. Further practice and discussion of different characters can help to extend the repertoire. At every opportunity, where a new or different character is introduced, talk about the sort of voice that might be used to convey that character. Try to record *Jackanory*. Many actors and actresses use a wonderful array of voices when reading the chosen story and these can form the basis of fruitful class discussions and at the same time provide excellent examples for the children. Encourage the children to think carefully about the character they wish to portray. Think in terms of sex, size and age. Also encourage them to decide what the characteristics of different animals might be: a lumbering elephant, a scurrying mouse, a sly fox or a cheeky monkey. Form the children into small groups and let them create their own character. Then, using only their voices, present this to the rest of the class. The dialogue spoken can be used to give clues but the rest of the class have to try to identify what sort of character is being portrayed. Ask the class or group questions, such as: How old is this character? What is it? How does it feel? Do you think it is big or small? Is the character from this country?

Practice of this kind will help the children to develop a repertoire of voices capable of showing a wide variety of characteristics which they can draw upon to create mood, atmosphere and interest when reading for themselves.

### Copymasters

Use **copymaster 34** (Voices) for the children to practise reading a simple text in a suitable way showing emotion and the ability to vary the pace and tone of the voice to suit the requirements of the text and character. Allow the children to interpret the character in whatever way they wish and encourage discussion of the suitability of the individual interpretations by the rest of the group.

**Area of study 2**

# PERSONAL RESPONSES

C35 –37

### Purpose

To encourage the children to form their own opinions of stories and poems.

### Materials needed

A selection of stories and poetry.

### Activity 1: Creating a sympathetic audience

In order to voice an opinion with any degree of confidence children need to feel that they will be listened to both by their peers and by you. They need to feel that what they have to say will be treated with respect and conversely they should be able to listen to others in the same manner.

It takes years to build up this mutual respect and the willingness to value the contribution of others but by the time children reach this level of reading ability and comprehension they should also be at the stage where they can work at this social level.

You can contribute to the continuing development of these skills by having regular discussion with the children. Any topic is appropriate as long as you give everyone an opportunity to speak, encouraging them to say what they feel and then making an appropriately positive response yourself. Try to get them to give reasons for their opinions and, by your own reaction, show the others that an individual opinion is neither right nor wrong but is what a person feels to be right, based on their impressions or understanding of facts. 'Everyone is entitled to their own opinion' is a maxim which surely holds an essential truth, but do also show the children that it is perfectly all right for others to disagree. However it is also important that they are shown how to voice disagreement courteously and without ridicule.

Try setting up a few role play situations to get over these conventions of good manners. You could use contrasts to illustrate the differences between courteous and discourteous disagreement. For example, get the children to try the following improvisations:

* two motorists discussing how their cars collided
* two children of their age deciding the ownership of a toy
* two children of their age deciding whose turn it is on the class computer
* a group of people on a bus deciding who should have the last seat.

**Different illustrative styles affect the text.**

## Activity 2: The qualities of a story

The qualities of a story which appeal to the listener could include:

- the story-line, which can be sad, exciting, funny, scary, adventurous, mysterious or ordinary
- the characters and how they are portrayed
- the subjects included, such as horses, trains, ghosts etc.
- the setting (snowy lands, dark cave, an ordinary house)
- the illustrations
- the writing style, which can be gripping, funny, descriptive or rude
- the ability to hold the reader's interest, which is closely related to the writing style and a combination of all the above.

As experienced readers who have already done some work on analysis, the children may be aware of these elements in a story but may not realise how they influence the reader. So spend some time discussing stories you have read together to try and highlight these features, possibly taking one session for each. During the discussions try to get the children to express what they feel about these things. Did they like them and, if so, what was it that appealed? Was it the language form used, the use of vocabulary or the descriptions? Was it the artists' interpretation of the story or the visual impact of the illustrations?

The writing style and the ability to hold the reader's interest are the two most difficult areas to explore. Try to read examples of different styles, even using some written for younger children. For example, Enid Blyton has a comfortable, chatty style; Rev. W. Awdry (*Thomas the Tank Engine*) has an authoritative, correct style; Roald Dahl uses language in a sharp, aggressive and excitable way and Rosemary Sutcliffe's style is beautifully descriptive. It is difficult but read short selections trying to highlight features about the style, such as short sentences, many descriptive words, lots of dialogue, use of dialect etc. and give your opinion. You can ask the children to say what they think about your ideas.

The ability to hold people's interest is a nebulous quality and in the main depends on personal preferences. Discuss with the children what it was that made them read on and finish the story. Did they want to find out what happened to the characters? Did they like the way the words sounded? Did they like the words used? Did they like the speed of the language? Was it the number of exciting events that made them read on?

Whatever part of the story you are discussing, encourage the children to identify what they liked and to think about what it was they found appealing and why. At this level they need to explore their preferences and to try to articulate them.

Use **copymaster 35** (A personal response) as a model for responding to any piece of writing. The children need to note what form the writing takes and its title, then make notes under the different headings (story-line, characters, subjects, setting, writing style, illustrations and ability to hold their interest) to say which aspects of the writing appealed to them and why.

## Activity 3: The qualities of a poem

A poem has some of the qualities of a story and some others too. A story is a piece of narrative prose but a poem can be a narrative or purely descriptive. A poem also differs in that it has a certain musical quality, it has a rhythm and it can rhyme. These qualities distinguish it from prose. Read and discuss a variety of poems with the children and discuss their personal responses in the same way as you did for stories but include rhyme and rhythm. How does this affect the sound of the reading? How does it make them feel? Does it contribute to the subject?

**Copymasters**
Use **copymaster 36** (My favourite bit) to give the children the opportunity to explore their responses to a poem or a story. The children have to write out their favourite part, illustrate it and then note down their response by giving brief reasons for their preferences.

Use **copymaster 37** (Night life) as a poem for the children to read and then note down which features they liked or disliked about it.

See also **copymasters 19 and 20**, which are review sheets on which children can write personal responses to books they have read.

 **Area of study 3**

# PREDICTION

 C38 –41

**Purpose**
To give the children practice in recognising those clues in a text which help the reader predict events.

**Materials needed**
A wide variety of books.

**Activity 1: Inference and deduction**
You can start to train the children to look for story-line clues at a very early stage, even before they start to read for themselves. As you read, stop at a point of action or imminent action and ask the children what they think might happen next. For example in *Thomas the Tank Engine* there might be this passage:

'Thomas climbed to the top of the slope and looked over the edge. He had the dreadful feeling that his wheels were slipping on the rails, even though driver had the brakes hard on. He felt the naughty trucks pushing him on, on, on!'

We might be correct to think that he is about to slip over the edge and race down the slope, but we need to look for facts to support this. The give-away clues are the straightforward statements that the train is on top of a slope, his wheels are slipping and he is being pushed. The reader or listener can deduce that Thomas will indeed go over the edge. However we can also read between the lines and infer that the trucks are delighted by the prospect and Thomas is not. We can say this because we have read that the trucks are 'naughty' so we can assume they are pushing him on purpose. The words, 'on, on, on' seem to be the victorious shout of the trucks as they succeed. The repetition makes this sound like dialogue from the trucks. Thomas's, 'dreadful feeling' tells us he is unhappy and knows he will go over the edge. We also know from past experience of these characters in this story that the troublesome trucks have already played several successful tricks on Thomas. Past experience of the characters in other stories tells us Thomas will get his own back.

We have used inference, deduction and past reading experience to analyse this short passage. From an early age ask the children to tell you what they think will happen and try to get them to give you evidence for this from the text. At level 4 the children may be quite good at this by unconsciously assimilating the clues but they need to identify the particular clues in order to help them with future more difficult analysis. Get them to look for facts which are presented either in narrative or dialogue form from which they can make deductions. Encourage them to think in these terms: 'We know this happened because it says exactly that here in the text'. Inferred feelings or happenings are more difficult to identify but get the children to use a formula such as, 'We think this might be the case because we read that . . .' and then to give the evidence for their assumption, possibly highlighting which vocabulary was particularly evocative. For example 'The little child spoke quietly and with a tiredness about her,' implies a sadness about the child. If this were in the story of the Little Match Girl and we had read about the death of the grandmother we might assume the child was missing her.

It would obviously spoil the story to continually stop and quiz the children, but if it is done occasionally it does serve to focus their minds on the story-line and the clues for future action. Stop at a dramatic point, have a quick chat about what everyone thinks might be the outcome and then quickly read on to see who was right. At another time, as a separate exercise, you can go into a more detailed analysis of a passage or story to give the children the skills to use in their own reading or listening. Use the following activity.

## Activity 2: Prediction exercises

The children are given a short passage to read which stops after a significant dramatic point or just as one is about to happen. The idea is that the children read, analyse and try to predict the outcome of events based on the evidence they have been given. This can be recorded verbally, as a drawing or in written form. It is a particularly good exercise for pairs or small groups for in-depth discussion, but can also be done with the whole class to introduce the technique. It can be presented as a series of passages which unfold a whole story. The children have to try to predict the outcome of a passage, then read the next passage which provides the answer and then predict the next part of the puzzle and so on.

Use **copymaster 38** (Prediction exercise) which gives the children an unknown passage to analyse. They can present their interpretation as a picture, in written form or as a discussion. In a single passage such as this, with a given set of facts, there could be several ways the action could be taken, each one correct. Do get the children to justify their reasons for a particular course of action based on the given situation.

Use **copymaster 39** (Once more, Ultraman!). This time the children are presented with a very well-known type of character who is put into a situation which causes him some problems. Knowing how a superhero usually behaves, the style of language used and, based on the facts given to them in the passage, the children have to resolve his difficulty.

Use **copymaster 40** (The secret of Dark Towers) as an example of an extended prediction exercise. This time the children read the first passage, discuss it and decide on the likely outcome given the facts presented. Then they are given the second passage which presents the author's ideas and they can then compare the two. (Their own are not necessarily wrong if they are based upon the facts.) Now, based upon the reading of the second passage – not their own ideas this time – they try to predict what the next part of the story will be and then it is presented to them to discuss as before. This story is left in an unresolved state so that the children can, as a separate exercise, finish it themselves.

This sheet can either be photocopied and cut up to present the children with the separate episodes or instead, two of the episodes can be blocked off with sheets of paper while each one is photocopied separately at the top of the sheet. In this case the children could write down on that sheet what they think will happen next in the story and then go on to read the next episode.

## Activity 3: Cloze procedure

This is a simple technique to encourage the reader to search the text to find clues about the identity of words missing from the text. It encourages careful, close reading with attention to detail. It also encourages the reader to scan ahead in the text from the point being read. This is useful when reading dialogue to ascertain the identity of the speaker or the manner of delivery. Pick a passage from a book or write a passage of suitable reading level. Classically every tenth word should be cut from the text, leaving a line or space for the reader to see. The reader then attempts to fill in the missing word. In some cases, especially if the missing word is an adjective, there may be several words which would be appropriate. For example,

'The _____ beast moved its head slowly from side to side knocking _____ trees with each sweep.'

'Down' is easy to guess for the second missing word as it forms part of a common combination but we know that the beast is so big it can knock down trees with its head so we can choose one of several descriptive words for the first word, such as, huge, gigantic, massive, monstrous or enormous. It is important to get the children to read all through the passage first to get the gist of the content. They will be able to guess any simple conjunctives and other syntactical omissions but will need to read backwards and forwards carefully to decide on some words which define the quality of something, such as the beast above.

You could read out the following short passages missing out the words printed in bold type and discuss with the children what the missing words might be:

a) Then all at **once** she felt something cold and **slimy** crawling over her feet.
b) The huge diamond **flashed** in the sunlight, a thousand colours **glittering** on its surface.
c) The most **delicious** smell floated from the **open** kitchen window. It was like chocolate pudding, roast **meat**, ice cream and buttered toast all **rolled** into one.
d) Slowly the **gigantic** machine rolled over the edge, its **metal** tracks grinding the loose rocks into dust as it **moved**.

Another value of this exercise is that it can be done collaboratively by two children who can discuss the exercise.

Use **copymaster 41** (Put in the missing words) as an example of a simple cloze procedure exercise. The children have a set of visual clues in the illustration, which could help them with some of the missing words.

It was dark but not quiet in the forest _____ night as our intrepid heroes began their fateful journey _____ the unknown. Fearlessly they pushed into hostile undergrowth. They _____ wildly at branches and leaves alike. Suddenly they heard a _____ noise. They froze in their tracks and _____ at each other. The noise came ...

terrific   sinister   dreadfully
quickly   slight
fearfully

# USING CATALOGUE SYSTEMS

C42
–48

## Purpose
To give pupils practice in using the various cataloguing systems of libraries, and also to give practice in search reading.

## Activity 1: Looking for books and magazines using a cataloguing system
All libraries have some method of cataloguing the books on their shelves. This makes it easier to find books as they are needed and also to replace the books on the shelves when they are returned. Most primary school libraries store this information in small filing cabinets which hold cards bearing the name of the book and the author under a chosen subject heading. They may also have a list of the authors in alphabetical order and this time the cards will show the name of the author plus a list of all the titles of books he or she has written and which are held by the library. In order to save time when looking for specific books, the children should be able to read this type of catalogue and then, provided they have some knowledge of how the library is arranged (see pp. 34–5), they should be able to go to the appropriate shelves and look for the book they need. In a school library there are many different ways of cataloguing. Some schools use a colour coding system, that is, using a different coloured label on the spine of each book and then arranging the books under broad subject headings such as History, Geography, Science, Nature and the Arts. Other schools use a simplified version of the Dewey Decimal Classification. This is where the nonfiction books are divided up into ten main groups. Each group is represented by figures on the spines of the books. The idea is to make the books easy to find. This system allows for the books to be placed numerically on the shelves so that if a child wishes to look for a particular book they can check for its number in the catalogue and then, by checking the numbers on the spines of the books, find the exact place where the book should be. If it is not there, they can safely assume that the book is already out on loan.

Use **copymaster 42** (The Dewey system) to give the children practice in deciding in which category certain books may be found. The ten main groups of books are printed at the top of the copymaster. The children have to look at the list of titles and decide in which category them might find them. They are to write the number and the category title in the space provided.

## Activity 2: Using a database and microfile
Most public libraries store their catalogue information on database or microfile. Since the rules governing the access to such systems vary from library to library it is suggested that you take the children to the library and arrange with the librarian a session to show the children how the system works. Make sure that they have a set of relevant questions to ask if they are searching for a particular book (name of author, title, publisher, subject heading) and try to ensure that each child has the opportunity to search for the book they need. They can follow up the activity by actually using the information they extract from the catalogue to search the shelves for the book. If they write out the details on a sheet as shown below they can use them as a ready reference.

## Activity 3: Obtaining information from outside sources
There are many firms and public companies who prepare fact sheets, posters and work cards for use when pursuing a particular line of study. Organisations such as Britoil, North Sea Gas, Powergen, Milk Marketing Board, Worldwide Fund for Nature, Greenpeace and the National Trust all have a good selection of posters and information packs. Addresses of these and other sources are to be found in *Treasure Chest for Teachers*, and many posters and charts are available from Pictorial Charts Educational Trust, 27 Kitchen Road, Ealing, London, W13 OUD. By encouraging the children to write off for their own information you can bring in many other aspects of the curriculum and it also makes

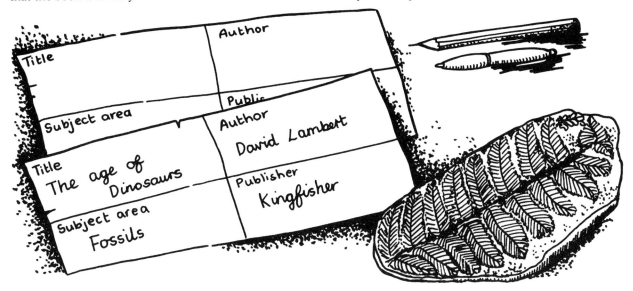

Look at the picture. What is the main point?

① a. The boat is sinking.
   b. The sun is shining brightly.

② a. Someone has been knocked down.
   b. A woman is looking in a shop window.

them aware that there are many other sources of information apart from the usual ones which can often give a more up-to-date account of trends, developments and information.

Use **copymaster 43** (Where will I find?) as a matching exercise in order to help the children to know where to go to find information. The children look at the list of things to find, and match them to the list of books and places where they may find the information they require.

**Activity 4: Search reading**
Once the children have found the books they need they will need to be able to extract the information quickly and effectively. To this end they will need to be aware of the two types of reading: full reading and search reading. The latter is more commonly referred to as skimming and scanning. When search reading they do not need to read every single word of text, but rather search quickly down the lines of words in order to find the information they need. This helps to save time, particularly in a library, when the children need this skill in order to extract relevant information quickly from reference books, or even be able to go through the books in order to see whether they actually do contain enough useful information for their requirements so that they can be read fully, at leisure, later on.

Use **copymaster 44** (Spot it). The children are to look at the picture and try to answer the questions as quickly as they can. They can simply write the answers as numbers alongside the questions.

Use **copymaster 45** (Take your pick). The children are to look at the pictures of individual items in the top set of illustrations. Then by taking one item at a time glance very quickly over the other pictures at the bottom and try to see which one contains the item they are looking for.

Use **copymaster 46** (Telephone directory). The children are to look at the extract from a telephone directory and then look at the sentences below. As quickly as they can they are to try to put in the missing details. For example, Joan Smith's telephone number is

061 ____ 3412. The answer would be 442.

You can give the children practice in skimming passages by asking them to find out how many times certain words appear. They are to take one word at a time.

Often we need to pick out the most important point from a number of ideas and as an introduction to this we can take a set of pictures and ask the children to decide what is the main point of each picture.

If we look at the picture on the right above, we can see that a woman is looking in a shop window and that there is a road accident. The main point of the picture is that a person has been knocked down by a car. Give the children sets of pictures of a similar kind and ask them to decide what is the main point of the picture.

Once they have understood this, give them some simple sentences and ask them to decide what is the main thing each sentence is saying, for example:

John was glad that he had been able to buy the book he needed because he had been afraid that the shop had sold out.

a) John was able to buy the book.
b) John had been afraid the shop had sold out of the book he needed.
The answer is a).

Give the children practice in scanning for individual words by moving their eyes rapidly over the print.

Use **copymaster 47** (Scanning) to give the children practice in scanning an index. The children are to imagine that this is an index list from a book about sport. They must look at the questions and see which sport is mentioned. Then, remembering the name of the sport, they glance quickly down the index until they find it, and write down the number of the page on which the information can be found.

Use **copymaster 48** (Search reading) to give practice in this skill. Try to see who can complete the task as quickly and as accurately as possible. The children read the question then, by search reading, look for that part of the text which contains the information they need to answer it.

# Attainment target 2: Reading

The development of the ability to read, understand and respond to all types of writing, as well as the development of information-retrieval strategies for the purposes of study.

| Level 5 | Statements of attainment | Example |
|---|---|---|
| | Pupils should be able to: | |
| | a) demonstrate, in talking and writing about a range of stories and poems which they have read, an ability to explain preferences. | *Make simple comparisons between stories or poems; offer justification for personal preference.* |
| | b) demonstrate, in talking or writing about fiction, poetry, non-fiction and other texts that they are developing their own views and can support them by reference to some details in the text. | *Discuss character, action, fact and opinion relating them to personal experience.* |
| | c) show in discussion that they can recognise whether subject matter in non-literary and media texts is presented as fact or opinion. | *Look for indications which suggest the difference: whether evidence is offered or whether persuasion is used in the absence of facts.* |
| | d) select reference books and other information materials and use organisational devices to find answers to their own questions and those of others. | *Decide what information is required for a project on a topic of their own choice and locate it by reference to chapter titles, subheadings, typefaces, symbol keys, etc.* |
| | e) show through discussion an awareness of a writer's choice of particular words and phrases and the effect on the reader. | *Recognise puns, word play, unconventional spellings and the placing together of pictures and text.* |

 **Area of study 1**

# JUSTIFYING PREFERENCES

 C49

## Purpose
To give the children practice in justifying personal preferences.

## Materials needed
A selection of newspapers and magazines which feature any type of book reviews, a selection of stories, poems and children's comics.

## Activity 1: Simple comparisons
In order to make comparisons of poems or stories the children need to work to a simple formula of analysis. They should read the piece two or three times to themselves and then read it with the following headings in mind, possibly making notes. The areas to look at are:

- subject
- presentation
- characterisation
- plot
- style
- use of language

- readability
- that sometimes indefinable quality which makes us read on and is a combination of all the above features.

As a simple exercise in comparisons the children should work on three short contrasting passages. Give them a chance to do this alone and in small groups. Their findings can be reported verbally or in notes (see example overleaf).

## Activity 2: Explaining preferences
As they read the passages for the activity above the children will enjoy some more than others and, because they are working to an assortment of headings, they will be able to associate their preferences to a particular feature in the writing. This should give them a starting point as they attempt to explain why they like one piece of writing more than another.

At this level they should be aware already of many of their personal preferences in life generally and in this activity they just need to apply these preferences to what

He saw the half-naked priests, Midir among them and behind the priests, the body of the King, borne by six of his warriors. The King's face was bare of the great wolfskin mantle that wrapped him round, his red hair fallen back, bright and ragged as the flare of the torches. There was a small terrible smile on his face and the same smile was stamped upon the painted face of one of the men who bore him: a very young warrior, with the same bright ragged hair, the same great beak of a nose, so that Drem knew, though no-one told him, that he was looking at father and son, the old King and the new King, yesterday's and tomorrow's.

*Warrior Scarlet* by Rosemary Sutcliff, Oxford University Press

Title : Warrior Scarlet

Presentation: written from boy's point of view

Subject : funeral of Warrior King

Plot : Drem - boy - watching funeral - thinking.

Characterisations : warriors - grand, strong.
King was strong - wolfskin mantle - symbol of strength
King - bright, ragged hair - unusual to look at - grand.

Use of language: simple words
strong words - ragged
flare
warrior
king
terrible

Readability: exciting, very easy to read, long sentences.

'Cool it, Grandma,' George said. But he got a bit of a shock when he saw smoke coming out of her nostrils. Clouds of black smoke were coming out of her nose and blowing around the room.
'By golly, you really are on fire,' George said.
'Of course I'm on fire,' she yelled. 'I'll be burned to a crisp! I'll be fried to a frizzle! I'll be boiled like a beetroot!'

*George's Marvellous Medicine* by Roald Dahl, Johnathan Cape and Penguin Books

Daniel

strange idea! fire inside Gran

words funny - frizzle, boiled, crisp
George funny - talking to Grandma
I like the saying - " Cool it, Grandma," we say
it - it annoys Dad!

44

they like about the writing. For example, a child might say, 'I enjoyed this book because it was really funny and I always like a good laugh. I've liked slapstick since I was very little and the action in the story is a bit like that. The characters are loud and funny too.' Encourage them to make notes or a mental list of things they liked about a story and things they disliked too. They need to be able to justify these opinions and to make reference to the text if necessary. 'The story was funny because of the language used by the characters, for example . . . ' The justification for liking a piece of writing can be as simple as, 'I liked this because it made me laugh/cry/feel frightened/think.' The important thing is that the child makes his or her own choice.

Give them plenty of opportunity to explain their own choices and preferences to a partner, a small group, the class or to you. Familiarity with a technique makes it easier to approach and sometimes at this age children are beginning to become self-conscious and so a little reluctant to explain themselves in public even though they may be able to do so quite well.

### Activity 3: Read some literary criticism
Bring in a selection of magazines and papers from the *Sun* to the *Times Literary Supplement* and *Child Education* and read or let the children read some of the reviews. Discuss the reviews and their impact and significance.

### Activity 4: Role play
To provide an opportunity to explain literary preferences organise a book programme as seen on television, with a panel or 'experts' and a selection of books. The rest of the class can make the choice or you can use this as an opportunity to publicise new books. Introduce it as a regular monthly event, changing the panel, of course.

### Copymasters
Use **copymaster 49** (Book review) for the children to write their own reviews, which you can collate into your own 'Literary Times'. It is presented in the form of a newspaper and the children can write in column spaces.

Area of study 2

# SKILLS OF CRITICISM

### Purpose
To give the children the opportunity to look at and discuss a variety of texts and relate them to personal experience.

### Activity 1: Looking at a variety of texts
When we talk about a variety of texts it is important to think in terms of all the different sorts of texts that the children are likely to come across in school and at home. These include:

- stories – fact, fantasy, fairy stories
- nonfiction of all types
- poetry (rhyming, blank verse)
- instructional reading (repair manuals, cookery books)
- posters
- magazines and comics.

Organise a display of as many different types of books, magazines and newspapers as you can find.

You may start off with a book they have read and ask them what they thought about the behaviour of the characters: Did the characters behave in a predictable way? Would they have behaved in a similar way themselves in a similar situation? Have they had a similar experience?

You can discuss all these points with the children and allow them to compare their own experiences and contrast their individual reactions.

The children can compare nonfiction books by collecting together different books on the same topic. They can compare the presentation of material by different authors and publishers, by looking at the way the information is presented, the use and style of the illustrations, the accessibility of the information and

the readability of the text. If there are several books the children can place them in order of preference.

They can compare poems on similar themes. Try to collect several poems about the sea or the countryside. Try to include several rhyming ones and several in blank verse and discuss with the children their preferences and first impressions. Ask the children to think about these points: How has the poem been written? Do the lines of the poem help them to form a picture in their mind? Have the children got similar memories of a time spent by the sea, or in the country? Which parts of the poem(s) do the children like most? What is it about a poem that they do not like? Can they give reasons?

Collect together several newspapers and try to find the same story reported by different reporters. Ask the children to look for similarities and differences. They can make separate lists. Ask them to compare figures contained in the reports and see if there are any discrepancies in them. You can video the news on the television and contrast the newspaper reports with that. The children can relate their own experiences in some instances, for example if an exciting event happens in their own town and they have first-hand experience of it, they can compare that with a report in the media and discuss the reasons for any differences or omissions. In discussions encourage the use of such phrases as 'It says here that . . . but I think . . . ' or 'I have found that . . . '

---

 **Area of study 3** | # FACT OR OPINION |  C50 –52

## Purpose
To give children an opportunity to look at and discuss non literary and media texts to try and distinguish between fact and opinion.

## Materials needed
A wide selection of texts, adverts, comics, newspapers and books.

## Activity 1: Distinguishing between fact and opinion
When we describe something in an approving or disapproving way we show our attitude towards it. We might say, for example, 'I think it is very nice to sit in the garden and sunbathe. This is my opinion, but other people may think differently.' At other times we may state things, such as 'Yesterday the highest temperature recorded was 21° Centigrade.' This is a fact not just an opinion because the temperature could be measured and found to be correct. Therefore it is not just something that someone thinks. Give the children a selection of different texts such as a telephone directory, a cookery book, a holiday brochure, or a leaflet advertising a new car. Ask them to sort them into those texts which deal in facts and those which also contain opinions. Discuss with them the reasons for placing a text in a particular category.

To give the children practice in recognising the difference between fact and opinion, discuss many different situations where fact and opinion may be expressed and then give them some pairs of sentences and ask them to decide which one is about what someone thinks, that is, an opinion. Read out the questions and ask the children to write the number of the question and then, after you have given the two alternatives, write 'a' or 'b' alongside it to indicate which one they think is an opinion.

1  a) Easter is the best time of year.
   b) Easter day was on 31, March 1991.
2  a) Mary is in the church choir.
   b) Mary is the best girl singer.
3  a) Peter's garden is the biggest in the street.
   b) Peter's garden is the most beautiful in the street.
4  a) Dogs are better than cats as pets.
   b) Sarah has a dog and two cats.

A good indication of opinion is when the person is describing things as beautiful, ugly, fine or best. This shows that the person is giving an opinion as someone else may disagree and use different describing words.

Use **copymaster 50** (Fact or opinion). The children are to look at the range of sentences then decide whether they are facts or opinions. They indicate this by writing the correct word at the end of each sentence in the space provided. They can also underline in the sentences those words which they think are opinions.

## Activity 2: Looking for bias
Sometimes when people state a fact they do so in such a way that they try to influence the reader or listener, for example different people can state the same thing in an entirely different way. Fact: a bronze figure was sold for £300. One person may report it like this, 'A very fine bronze figure was sold for the very low price of £300.' Another person may report the same thing in this way: 'A remarkably high price of £300 was paid for a rather poor bronze figure'. There is a bias in favour of the figure in the first report since the writer uses words such as 'very fine' and 'very low price' to influence his reader. In the second report the bias is against the figure because the writer uses such words as 'remarkably high price' and 'rather poor' to make the reader think less favourably about it. Use other examples like this to show the children that when they are reading so-called factual reports they have to be aware of bias and persuasion. Encourage them to collect newspaper reports of football matches and look for evidence of bias in these.

Use **copymaster 51** (For and against) to give the children practice in deciding whether the text is for or against the subject. They are to look at the statement of fact, and then look at the two reports following it. After reading the reports they are to indicate by colouring in the appropriate box to show whether they think the report is biased for or against.

### Activity 3: Persuasion

Some public information films and advertisements use persuasion to get their message across to certain members of high risk groups. For example, the 'Smoking can damage your health' campaign did not rely on government statistics to shock people into giving up smoking, but relied upon the anti-social aspect of it to try and persuade people to give up. Similarly with anti-drugs campaigns the emphasis has been on persuasion through films showing the horrors of the effects of drugs on the lives of young people, rather than by showing statistics. In both cases it was felt that situations with which people could identify would be far more effective than showing a set of comparatively meaningless figures.

Use **copymaster 52** (Advertisement) for the children to devise an advertising message to persuade people to buy a pain relief product. The sheet can also be used to devise a message that misuse of drugs can be very harmful. The sheets can be used to set up a display to highlight the use and misuse of drugs.

 Area of study 4

# FINDING INFORMATION

 C53 –54

### Purpose

To decide what information they need for their own topic work and locate it.

### Activity 1: Deciding areas of study for individual topics

Discuss with the children the range of individual topics they might wish to study. Then ask them to write down a set of questions they might ask in order to give the best information about their chosen topic. They might wish to make a topic web as shown below.

When completed discuss each web with each child to ensure optimum coverage. The next step is to go along to the library and start looking for the books they need. The activities mentioned in the previous levels of this attainment target should ensure that the children know how to use the library and its catalogue system, and once they have found the books they need their attention should focus now upon locating the exact information they need. After using the index and contents list they will be directed to the relevant part of the book. Within that part they will need to make use of chapter titles and sub-headings which they can look for as they search read the pages.

Use **copymaster 53** (Fascinating facts) to help the children look for sub-headings in a page of text. They will need a set of encyclopedias and they are to choose one volume. They can open it anywhere. They do not need to read it but just let their eye run down the page, scanning to see if they can spot anything really interesting. When they find something that really catches their eye they are to stop and read it carefully. If it is not really interesting, they go on scanning, but if it is interesting they copy it out in the space provided. They are then to record the source so that if someone does not believe them they can look it up for themselves.

### Activity 2: A strategy for approaching topic work

a) Decide on the topic. The first objective is to understand any terms with which they may not be familiar and for this they will need to consult a

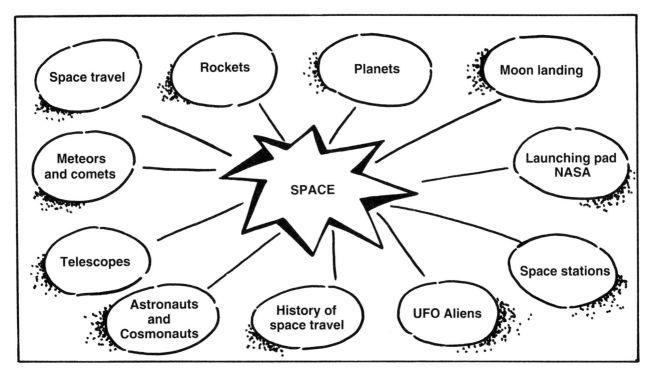

dictionary. they can make a list of these terms and write their definitions alongside.

b) Make a list of key word search terms. If the children are studying castles, for example, they may need a list like this:

Defendable sites and locations

Castles through the ages, hill-top forts, Roman forts, Norman castles, Medieval castles, Tudor castles

Castle architecture–towers, battlements, portcullis, motte, bailey, dungeon, gatehouse, barbican, curtain wall

Life in a castle (choose one or two periods)

Ruined castles

Castles today

Famous castles

c) Check the search items against the subject index in the library and then check the classified cards to see how many books the library has on the chosen topic. The children can list them by making a note of the Dewey number, the author, and the title.

d) Check the shelves. The children then list the suitable books when they have skimmed through them looking at the contents list, index and illustrations. They can also make a note of useful pages, chapters and illustrations as they go along.

e) Check for any other sources of information. Are there any addresses the children can write to for further information about a particular aspect of their topic? Look for posters, photographs, magazines and filmstrips.

f) Note taking. Try to encourage the children to note the most important facts by reading the text, several times if necessary, then they are to close the book and try to write down as much as they can remember. They can draft and re-draft until they arrive at their best effort. This will reduce the prospect of wholesale copying of text from books.

Use **copymaster 54** (Research) to choose an area of study concerning famous people or inventions and, using encyclopedias, nonfiction books or magazines, to try to find out as much as possible about it.

 **AREA of study 5** | # AWARENESS OF LANGUAGE USE  C55

## Purpose

To foster an awareness of the writer's choice of words and illustrations and their effect on the reader.

## Materials needed

A variety of stories and poems illustrated in as many styles as possible.

## Activity 1: Picture/text match

Look at a great variety of illustrated books and notice the following features:

- the style, colours and size of illustration
- the frequency of illustration
- the match of picture and text.

Working in small groups to allow maximum participation in discussion, explore the children's preferences for style, encouraging them to make their own judgements and to recognise that individuals can have widely differing opinions about the same thing.

You can then go on to discuss the suitability of the illustrations for the story, discussing such things as: does the illustration detract interest from the story or add something to it by making a visual comment? Is the illustration in the right place in that it is next to the part of the text it portrays? What would its effect be if the same illustration was in a different place? Do you think the style suits the story, for example, would a racy cartoon style such as Quentin Blake's (used in the Roald Dahl books) suit an adventure or a comedy story? Can you think of a better subject for an illustration in a particular place? Is the colour and size important in this context? Do you like the illustrations in the story?

Use **copymaster 55** (Illustration) to help the children think about these points. They are given a short piece of text and asked to do an illustration for it. Then they are given an illustration and asked to try to write a piece to fit it.

Alternatively, give the children a short printed text and a double-page spread of paper and ask them to cut up the text and fit it on the pages with suitable illustrations.

## Activity 2: Jokes

This is classic use of word play for humour's sake. Get the children to write down as many jokes as they can think of, then have a joke-telling session. As well as having fun, try to decide afterwards what made the jokes funny or not. Was laughter inspired by the subject or by the use of particular words, the sound of the words or an image inspired by the words? It is often a combination of these elements but if you try to sort the jokes into those which are funny just because of clever use of words and those which rely on an almost slapstick image, then the children will at least have had their attention focused on one important use of language.

For example:

'Why do you need holes in your trousers?'

'To put your legs through!'

This creates a funny image of trousers without leg holes.

'What happened to the boy who slept with his head under the pillow?'

'The fairies took away all his teeth!'

This is another funny image.

'If a buttercup is yellow, what colour is a hiccup?'
'Burple!'
This is a play on the words 'burp' (always funny for children and adults!) and 'purple'.

'What did the electrician's wife say when he came home late?'
'Wire you insulate?'
This is a pun! The dictionary definition of a pun is, 'Humorous use of a word to suggest different meanings.'

'Where did Humpty Dumpty put his hat?'
'Humpty dumped 'is 'at on the wall!'
This is another play with words relying on unconventional spelling and perhaps needs to be appreciated visually.

Look at limericks and riddles too. Read poems and jokes by writers such as Michael Rosen, Ted Hughes, Spike Milligan, Edward Lear, Hilaire Belloc, Robert Louis Stevenson and A. A. Milne.

You may like to make a topic out of jokes and humour and look into what makes people laugh. Is humour culturally based and therefore linked to language or is there a universal humour? Children from ethnic minorities or those children who have travelled abroad a lot may be able to help here. Can humour be purely visual, such as in the old slapstick silent films of Charlie Chaplin and Laurel and Hardy, the out-takes on programmes such as *It'll be all right on the night* and amateur video out-takes on *You've been framed*?

### Activity 3: The effect of words
Ask the children to find or bring in their favourite books and then have a session of looking through them, in pairs or small groups, to find ways in which language is used to create excitement, fear, humour, sadness and anticipation.

For example, look for strategies such as use of punctuation or capital letters or even different lettering to create an effect. Discuss what this effect is. What is the effect on the reader of the following, for example:

'The wolf began to howl and this turned into an unearthly

'No' he said firmly and then, 'NO, NO, NO!!!' as he tore open the parcel.

Look for evocative names such as, 'Hardlock House' and 'Captain Grimthorpe' in Shirley Hughes's, *It's too frightening for me*. Would the house be more welcoming and the villain less frightening if they were named differently? Can the children find some names of funny, strong, weak or frightening characters or places? Ask why these names have these qualities. Is it because they have them embedded in the structure of the name, such as Grimthorpe? Is the name illustrative of the behaviour of the character? For example, 'Bodger' the incompetent caretaker, 'Miss Moon' the light-headed, far-away deputy head and 'Mrs Trout' the cold, hard-headed teacher in the children's TV series, *Bodger and Badger*.

Discuss use of dialogue, looking at extracts from work by C.S. Lewis and Roald Dahl. Grand characters like Aslan use a fairly simple speech form, whereas The Grand High Witch employs a mock European accent, produced by unconventional spelling, 'Rrree moof your masks!' she shrieks. Discuss how the qualifications of dialogue like, 'shriek, yells, explained, answered calmly, snapped' also work to develop the character and the plot. Does the writer use accent and dialect for some characters and why?

Look at use of description and the words used to create a scene. Get the children to find descriptive passages from their books and then discuss how the words used help to build up a picture.

At this level of Key Stage 2 it is sufficient to introduce the children to an awareness of these language features and give them some experience of discussing them in order to make their reading more enjoyable and effective.

## Organisational material for reading
The following copymasters are included to aid you in the general organisation of reading on a practical level.

Use **copymaster 56** (Books) as a child's personal record of reading in school.

Use **copymaster 57** (Awards 1) as examples of awards to present for progress.

Use **copymaster 58** (Awards 2) either as a record of a child's reading or as a combined award, which could be displayed for others to see.

Use **copymaster 59** (Book week) as a poster for a Book Week event. This can be enlarged to A3 size.

Use **copymaster 60** (Great new titles in our library) as a poster to advertise new books.

## Attainment target 3: Writing

A growing ability to construct and convey meaning in written language matching style to audience and purpose.

| Level 3 | Statements of attainment | Example |
|---|---|---|

**Pupils should be able to:**

a) produce, independently, pieces of writing using complete sentences, mainly demarcated with capital letters and full stops or question marks.

b) shape chronological writing, beginning to use a wider range of sentence connectives than 'and' and 'then'.

*but when after so because*

c) write more complex stories with detail beyond simple events and with a defined ending.

*Stories which include a description of setting and the feelings of characters.*

d) produce a range of types of non-chronological writing.

*Plans and diagrams, description of a person or place, or notes for an activity in science or design.*

e) begin to revise and redraft in discussion with the teacher, other adults, or other children in the class, paying attention to meaning and clarity as well as checking for matters such as correct and consistent use of tenses and pronouns.

## SENTENCES

C61 –71

**Introduction**

At first, writing is a shared experience with the teacher or another adult acting as scribe. The child dictates a comment about his or her picture then later, to establish ownership of the writing, the child is encouraged to trace write over the words. When hand–eye co-ordination develops further, he or she can copy write underneath. At this time the only audience the child perceives is himself and possibly the teacher, so to broaden this experience the teacher reads out a child's writing to the class. This is a great boost to self-esteem and begins to develop the idea of audience and give a purpose for writing. Our environment is crowded with writing for different purposes and the Key Stage 1 child is encouraged to enquire about them. Writing is introduced into play situations, classroom items are labelled, books are available and listening to stories and poems are part of the language experience. Language which is meaningful to the children is written down to help develop a sight vocabulary of words which is part of their language experience.

For continued development children need word building and decoding skills in order to make words for themselves. These words are grouped into phrases and then sentences. They need plenty of practice in writing material which is relevant to them and the correct

50

language example to help guide their thoughts into sentence form. Simple sentence workcards will provide a more formal practice situation to help them see sentences as complete units of meaning. For example, they select a word from a limited choice to complete a sentence (examples shown above).

They need to attempt simple comprehension exercises both using a picture as the object of enquiry and using a written passage.

At Key Stage 2 this same approach is necessary at Level 3. The children need continued purposeful opportunities for independent writing and, at the same time, formal practice of the combined skills of writing. For the purpose of this area of study we are looking at sentence structure.

## Purpose
To give the children practice in recognising and writing sentences.

## Materials needed
Old magazines, comics, card, pens, glue.

## Activity 1: Sentences make sense
A sentence is a string of words which make complete sense and tell us something meaningful. A phrase is a group of words that do not make any sense on their own such as, 'Where is a'. Sentences are demarcated by capital letters and full stops. Make some workcards showing a selection of sentences and phrases and ask the children to identify the sentences by copying them out and using the correct punctuation (see below).

They can then go on to make the phrases into complete sentences. Nouns and verbs are dealt with in the following activities. At this stage focus the attention on the sentence communicating some idea, meaning something.

Use **copymaster 61** (Sentences 1), **copymaster 62** (Sentences 2) and **copymaster 63** (Sentences 3) to give further practice in recognising and making sentences.

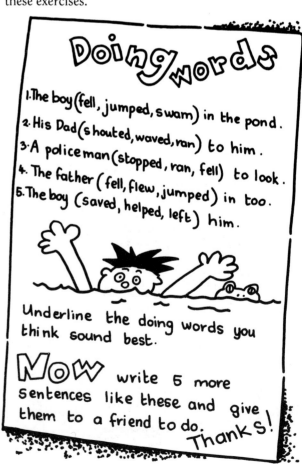

Doing words
Underline them.
I <u>run</u> all the way home.
I jump down the steps.
We all love school.
We shout with joy at home time.
We all dash home.

## Activity 2: Doing words

a) Play *What's my line* with verbs. Calling them 'doing words' at this stage seems a useful illustration of their purpose for the children. Make some large cards each with a different verb written on it but pick easily mimed actions, such as, hop, stretch, eat, drink, bend, carry, wave etc. Pick one child at a time to choose a card from the pack and then mime that action. The rest of the class have to guess the doing word which is held up for them to see if they guess correctly. The one who makes the correct guess is the next person to mime.

b) Make a list of doing words. Have a brainstorming session and try to think of as many doing words as possible. Write these on long strips of paper which you can join together to make the 'longest list in the world' and display on the classroom wall.

c) Make workcards or sheets which give the children some practice in identifying and using verbs. For example:

Picking the verb from simple sentences – 'I hate school.'

Finding a verb to fit into a sentence from a selection provided – 'The boy (ran, fell, rode) his bike to school.'

Using given verbs to form sentences of their own – riding, swimming, flying, stopping, falling, mended, picked, cleaned, watched, listened.

Put collections of verbs of the same tense together so that the children can develop a rhythm in their thinking and writing at this stage.

Use **copymaster 64** (Doing words 1), **copymaster 65** (Doing words 2) and **copymaster 66** (Doing words 3) for these exercises.

stamp
hit
run
walk
skip
draw
paint
write
read
enjoy
hate
love
kiss
cuddle
drink
eat
cook
buy
collect
sell
carry
fetch

Doing words

1. The boy (fell, jumped, swam) in the pond.
2. His Dad (shouted, waved, ran) to him.
3. A policeman (stopped, ran, fell) to look.
4. The father (fell, flew, jumped) to look.
5. The boy (saved, helped, left) him.

Underline the doing words you think sound best.

**Now** write 5 more sentences like these and give them to a friend to do. Thanks!

**Activity 3: Naming words**

At this level it is useful to use the term 'naming words' instead of 'nouns' while the subject is new, but you can quickly introduce the term noun and the sub-divisions of proper and common nouns.

Nouns are the names of things in a sentence and are easy to identify if you ask the children to apply a simple test. Try putting 'a', 'an' or 'the' in front of the word and if it makes sense then it is a noun. For example, you can say, a car, a bat, the cheese, an apple, but you cannot say, a happen, a dropped, the trying, an every.

Give the children a list of words and ask them to pick out the nouns.

Put the children into pairs or threes and have a nouns race. In a given time, for example one minute, ask the children to write down as many nouns as they can think of. Check them by getting the children to read them out and let the rest of the class help with the assessment. Take this one stage further and enlist the aid of a dictionary. Give each group a letter and ask them to find as many nouns beginning with that letter as they can in one minute.

Make cards or worksheets for noun recognition. The following activities are useful:

a) Write out a short, simple passage but leave a blank where the nouns should be. Use pictures from comics or magazines or some drawn by the children to illustrate it and provide clues as to the noun. Avoid proper nouns for this exercise.

b) Write out short sentences and ask the children to underline the nouns.

Use **copymaster 67** (Nouns 1) for both these activities.

Introduce proper nouns and common nouns. The rule is that all names of people, places and special things like days of the week or months begin with a capital letter and are called proper nouns. Other names start with small letters, except when they are the first word in a sentence and they are called common nouns.

a) Make lists of mixed nouns and ask the children to identify the proper nouns by writing them with an initial capital letter.

b) Write out sentences containing proper nouns with the initial capital letter missing from the nouns and ask the children to write these in.

c) Write out sentences with proper and common nouns and ask the children to underline all the nouns.

d) Ask the children to make lists of five nouns for each of a selection of subject headings: countries, girls'/boys' names, things to eat, clothes, etc.

Use **copymaster 68** (Nouns 2) for examples of these exercises.

### Activity 4: Picture comprehension

Using magazines and comics get the children to cut out some large pictures which appeal to them and are full of detail. Glue these to cards which are twice as deep so that you can write questions about the picture which require the reader to look carefully for details and which can be answered with a simple sentence. The aim is to get the children to think of a complete sentence for the answer and to use the correct punctuation conventions in a simplified writing situation. Hopefully they will, with practice, apply this to their own writing.

Use **copymaster 69** (Look carefully) as an example of this exercise. The children can write their answer underneath the question in the space provided.

### Activity 5: Reading comprehension

Using books of an appropriate reading level, select short passages or poems which contain a lot of detail and will be fruitful for questioning. Get the children to write out the passages on paper, type them on a word processor or photocopy them. Mount the passages onto card leaving room for questions and form questions based on the same criterion as for Activity 1. Encourage the children to keep referring to the passage of writing for the answer to the questions to train them to search for evidence at source.

Use **copymaster 70** (Read carefully) as an example of this exercise. In this case the children have to answer questions on a poem.

### Activity 6: Question marks

a) Making up questions. Let the children select some magazine pictures which appeal to them and which are full of detail. Ask them to make their own picture comprehension card. They can work with a friend to make up five questions. Encourage them to look for things in the picture that interest them and then make up a question about it, for example, 'Can you see the red seaweed?' 'Is the shark swimming towards the wreck or away from it?' If they do a first draft in rough you can check on the suitability of the questions for the picture and the reader. You can discuss any changes together. The children will already have read pieces using a question mark in other comprehension cards and now they have to use the question mark at the end of each of the questions they write.

b) Identifying questions. Make cards or worksheets which have short sentences, some of which are questions and some of which are statements. Ask the children to distinguish between them and put in the question marks. It is very helpful to let them work with a partner and read the sentences out loud.

Use **copymaster 71** (Questions) which has several examples of this exercise.

# CHRONOLOGICAL WRITING

C72 –73

## Purpose

To encourage children to shape their chronological writing by using a wider range of sentence connectives.

## Activity 1: Shaping chronological writing

When children have to report a series of events in a logical order or in a chronological way their concentration is focused largely upon getting the sequence correct. This usually results in a series of short sentences which, if they are joined together, are usually connected by the words 'and' and 'then'. In order to stress the over-use of these words, it will be necessary to write an account which really does over-use them. This will give the children an opportunity to observe this especially if you do it as an exercise in shared writing. They can then discuss, as a class, ways in which the account may be improved. An example might be:

'Maria was going for a picnic with her friend Sue, and she was going to take some salad and she got a large box and she put some lettuce in and some cucumber and some tomatoes and some sliced carrot and some radishes and she put the lid on the box and she went to the picnic.'

At this level the children should be in a better position to start thinking of other suitable words to connect the sentences or indeed to start to restructure the account completely in order to create a more complex single sentence from several simple ones.

The children can be grouped together in small groups to draft an outline of all the main events in the activity they wish to report. They can then produce their own sequence of events in chronological order and time can be given for a comparison between the different groups, in order to establish that all the groups have included the necessary details in the right order. This outline can be done in the form of rough notes, to save time, and the second stage is for the children to work together upon the creation of a more structured report. At this point you can focus their attention upon the way that the chronological details are joined together. Again give them an opportunity to present their ideas to the other groups and ask for suggestions from the other groups as to how the report may be improved. Discuss the range of appropriate joining words and try to identify any over-use of particular words. This can lead to a discussion of suitable alternatives. When each of the reports have been discussed in this way the children can then write up their report. Discussion of each group's draft gives the children an opportunity to see which words are most suitable for connecting the different sentences and it also helps them to become more familiar with the use of such words.

## Activity 2: Remembering the sequence of events

Give the children lots of exercises in ordering a sequence of events. These can be very simple, such as the steps to be followed when making a cup of tea or boiling an egg. You can present these as a series of pictures and the children have to place them in the correct order. Or you can actually perform a simple task and then ask the children to write down the step-by-step procedure.

This activity can be extended by adopting the same approach to simple Science experiments, Art and Craft techniques, or CDT projects. Remember to keep the task very simple and point out each important stage as it is reached. Give the children lots of practice in this until they can identify these points for themselves. After this the activities can become a little more detailed in order to develop the children's skills further. Discuss with the children the sort of information they will need to include when writing up the details of, for example, a Science experiment.

They will include:

- a list of materials and equipment used
- an indication of what they were trying to find out
- a step-by-step account of what they did
- a report of what happened at appropriate points in the experiment
- an attempt to explain with reasons what happened
- a summary of what they discovered.

As the children become familiar with this process of description and analysis you can encourage them to think about the range of sentence connectives they have used in their initial drafts and you can try to get the children to suggest alternatives if they feel that they have over-used 'and' and 'then'. A useful way of highlighting this is to use a tape recorder to record the children describing the activity. This can then be played back and the details and sequence of events noted. Discussion of the sentence connectives can then take place.

As an alternative to writing accounts of activities, another way of organising events in a chronological sequence is for the children to re-tell a familiar story or one that has just been read. The advantage of this is that the account can be compared with the original by the children themselves as a shared reading exercise.

Another way of doing this is to give the children a set of mixed up but connected sentences and ask them to place them in the correct order, as shown here.

Use **copymaster 72** (Sorting sentences) to give the children practice in arranging sentences in the correct chronological order. Each sentence is given a letter and the children have to write the correct sequence of sentences and then fill in the grid at the bottom of the sheet.

**Activity 3: Identifying alternatives to 'and' and 'then'**
Workcards can be used to give the children practice in the use of alternatives to 'and' and 'then'. Have sets of two sentences side by side and ask the children to connect them together using one of the words in the box at the bottom.

The children can then write out the new complete sentence, which will give them further practice in more complex sentence construction and, at the same time, help to extend their vocabulary of connecting words. As mentioned previously, try to include activities of this nature in other areas of the curriculum and not merely as exercises done out of context. By using such activities in a cross-curricular way the children will soon become familiar with a range of suitable alternatives and be more willing to use them in a wide variety of situations. Give the children lots of practice in recognising joining words by making cards with a range of different sentences which can be joined with words such as: but, either, or, neither, nor, because, as, so, unless and if. Other linking words can include: who, which, that and whom. Sometimes the sentence may have to be completely changed around in order to connect it in a different way.
For example:

The boy was not looking where he was going.
He fell and cut his leg.

These two sentences could be joined in a variety of ways but the most obvious way might be:

The boy was not looking where he was going, so he fell and cut his leg.

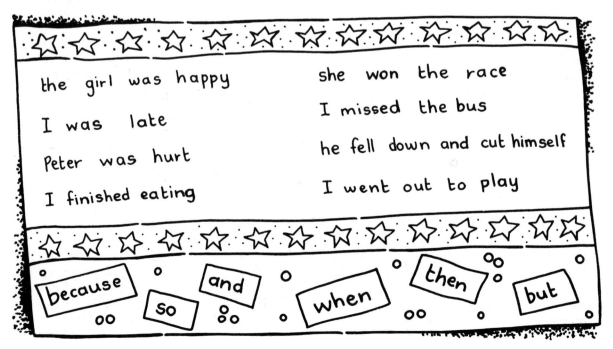

Other words could also have been used and you can discuss which ones the children would choose. You can then show them that the joining word need not always go in between the two sentences. Sometimes it can go at the beginning. If we use the word 'because' the sentence will now read:

Because the boy was not looking where he was going he fell and cut his leg.

This is a higher order skill and should only be introduced after a great deal of practice with the simpler examples. The word 'then' can be replaced with such words as 'next', 'soon', 'afterwards' or even simple phrases such as 'after a while', or 'soon after this'. Whenever conjunctions or sentence connectives are used, the children should be encouraged to vary the words as much as possible and try to avoid repeating the same word immediately a connective is needed. This will help the flow of the report and make it more interesting.

Use **copymaster 73** (Joining sentences) as an exercise in which the children look at the sentences and, from the bank of words below, choose the word they think most suitable to join them together.

 **Area of study 3**

# MORE COMPLEX STORIES

C74 –87

## Purpose
To give practice in writing detail beyond simple events.

## Materials needed
Old comics and magazines, scissors, glue, card, pens, a large selection of story books.

## Activity 1: Descriptions of characters
Read out a large selection of character descriptions and discuss with the children what sort of details are included. Some descriptions may be spread out within other details of the story. Some may be short, concise sentences containing advanced descriptive features such as use of adjectives and similes. Ask the children to try and visualise the character as they listen to a description and note that a description need not contain details of every aspect of a character to be effective. For example, 'He was black, wild and very hungry,' as a short description of a panther on the loose conjures up the image of a dangerous animal.

Read a few varied yet vivid descriptions and ask the children to draw what they visualise for each one. Compare the pictures together and let the children amend their pictures if they want to as a result of the discussion.

Use **copymaster 74** (Descriptions) for two exercises. First of all, let the children use the sheet in pairs to note down any features they can remember after having heard a description. This can include quotes. Secondly, use it for the children to make notes on, prior to writing their own description. They can use it to try out vocabulary, phrases and the general outline of the character. You could do the exercise together on an A3 photocopy to give them the idea.

Get the children to cut out pictures of characters that appeal to them from magazines, comics or old books. Ask them not to read any of the story associated with the pictures. Indeed the pictures need not be of characters from a work of fiction; they can be human, animal, vegetable, machines or even clouds of coloured light.

Spread the pictures on a table and ask the children to pick two very different ones. They can work in pairs to compose a description of their chosen characters, imagining any features of behaviour they wish to add. You should discuss with them the fact that beauty is not always associated with good behaviour and vice versa. If they select a terrifically ugly character it might behave kindly. Perhaps you could read the story of *Beauty and the Beast*. During the discussions about appearance the idea of beauty being in the eye of the beholder may also come up and you could discuss the children's notions of beauty.

Use **copymaster 75** (Wanted) for the children to produce a description of a criminal, a lost loved one or friend, a lost pet or toy. They can also draw a picture to accompany the description. This sort of description will need to have more detail than one within a story where a general impression can make great impact. In this case as much detail as possible will be needed to aid recovery of the lost one. See pp. 61–3 on non-chronological writing.

Use **copymaster 76** (My friend) to write a description and draw an accompanying picture of a friend. Ask the children to do this individually and not to reveal the identity of the subject. The descriptions can then be read out to the class to see if they can identify the mystery person. Later the names can be added and the sheets displayed to promote lively discussion about the accuracy of the writing. To give a little excitement to the displayed writing, cut the bottom of the sheet as shown overleaf, stick a piece of paper behind the opening and write the subject's name on here so that readers have to lift the flap to find out who it is.

## Activity 2: Feelings of characters
The feelings of characters and the behaviour which results from these feelings are often the very things that children relate to most easily in a story. They need to hear descriptions of feelings in order to appreciate the concept fully. Sometimes the descriptions may be merely a sentence, sometimes they may be longer and more detailed.

Look at the work of Roald Dahl and the traditional fairy stories such as *The Snow Queen* where the feelings of the characters strongly motivate the action. Kay was greedy and so followed the Snow Queen. Gerda, missing her friend and being totally loyal, followed to rescue him.

Pick a few well-known characters and discuss what their feelings were in their own story setting. For example, how did the Ugly Sisters feel when they got the invitation to the ball? How do we know this? How did the Wicked Queen feel when she found out that Snow White was still alive and remained her rival in beauty? How do we know this and what did she do about her feelings? What did the Seven Dwarves feel like when they found Snow White hurt? What were the Prince's feelings when he found her in the glass coffin? Read whole stories and afterwards discuss the characters' feelings at different times in the action. It will help if you introduce the exercise before the story reading by asking the children to listen out for the information needed. During your discussion make a point of referring to the text to check impressions and verify facts.

Make a sheet of questions about the feelings of characters from a selection of stories in your class library. You can either use these as exercises to be done with the books or write out the questions to be displayed as stimulus for children using the library and as a focus for their reading.

## Activity 3: Adjectives

Adjectives are the words we use to describe things; they modify nouns. You can explain this to the children by saying that they tell us more about the noun. There are many types of adjective but, at this stage, it is best to merely introduce those which answer the question, 'What kind of?' It seems appropriate to introduce the use of adjectives when working on descriptions.

The following simple exercises will help the children to grasp the concept if you use them in conjunction with this work and remind the children of their use when they are writing stories.

a) Matching nouns and adjectives. Working in groups or as a class write down two lists on the board, one of nouns and one of adjectives. Then work through the nouns trying different adjectives. Most will take several different adjectives with wildly differing and sometimes hilarious effects.

b) One noun can be changed in many ways. Cut out or draw a picture to illustrate a single noun, for example, an elephant. Next think of as many different adjectives as possible to describe this noun

Spotty pink elephant

Cross baby elephant

and change it. For example, large, small, old, young, spotty, wrinkled, grey, pink, inflatable, toy, wild, ferocious, baby, laughing, angry, fierce etc. Let the children pick one or two adjectives and draw the appropriate type of elephant.

c) Read a really short descriptive passage to the children and ask them to listen for adjectives and note them down as you read. You may need to read it a couple of times and then you can compare notes and write the words on the board. Re-read it so that the children are listening for the adjectives they have identified and can also see them on the board.

d) Give the children a short story which has no adjectives and ask the children to make it more interesting by adding an adjective for each noun. See **copymaster 79**.

e) Think up a list of ten adjectives to describe a person and write them on the board. Next ask the children to try to think of the opposite of each word. You can then ask them to think carefully and write down five words which best describe first themselves and then a good friend.

Use **copymaster 77** (Describing words) which asks the children to match nouns and adjectives and also to pick suitable adjectives from a selection to fit with given nouns and pictures.

Use **copymaster 78** (Adjectives 1) where the children have to make selections of adjectives to suit particular descriptions and also to identify the adjectives in a passage.

Use **copymaster 79** (Adjectives 2) for the children to complete a short story and some sentences by adding the adjectives.

Use **copymaster 80** (What did you say?) for the children to add an adjective to the nouns in the speech

bubbles, each of which describes one aspect of a party. This time they can use adjectives of their own if they do not want to use any of the ones provided.

**Activity 4: Adverbs**

A word that tells us more about the meaning of a verb is called an adverb and again there are many different kinds. At this level it is best to keep to the more obvious examples where a simple verb is directly affected: 'The star shone brightly.' You can do similar exercises to the ones used with adjectives.

a) Miming. Think of about ten action verbs and write them on the board. Next get a child to mime one of the actions, for example, stretching. Ask the children how she or he did this. Was the action done fast, slowly, quickly, daintily or jerkily? If you supply them with the first few examples of adverbs they will soon catch on. Use a different child to mime each verb and write the verb and its selection of adverbs in sets on the board.

b) Matching. Make two lists, one of action verbs and one of suitable adverbs. Discuss likely pairings with the children or let them work on this in small groups.

c) Pick one. Give the children a selection of simple sentences with no adverbs and a list of suitable adverbs which they have to fit in the sentences. This can be done as a group or class lesson.

Use **copymaster 81** (Adverbs 1) for the children to practise matching verbs and adverbs and also choosing suitable adverbs for a purpose.

Use **copymaster 82** (Adverbs 2) to give the children opportunity to think of suitable adverbs to fit in the given sentences.

## Activity 5: Settings

Read descriptions of settings. Find a selection of books which have a variety of styles and good descriptions of settings and read these to the children. Ask them to try to visualise the setting as they listen and discuss whether this gives them any inkling of what might happen in the story. For example, if the story opens with a howling blizzard in the Arctic wastes and a man and his sledge dogs huddled together for comfort and shelter, then the reader knows that the man and his dogs will be in some danger. The setting creates an atmosphere for the story.

The setting of a story is usually where and when the action takes place. Sometimes the action moves to different locations and times and if, for example, there is any element of science fiction or magic in the plot the time element may vary considerably. The story could be set at night, in the day, in the future, in the past, during one afternoon and so on. Ask the children to think of the stories they have read and TV and radio dramas they may have seen or heard and write down as a group a list of different times and places.

Ask the children to consider what effect a description of setting has on them. Does it make them want to read on? What descriptive words stick in their minds when they think of a setting from a story? Then ask them to write a description. Choose one of the locations and times from the list they made above and discuss what it might be like. Write all the descriptive words you can think of as a class on the board and then let the children put it together as a very short description.

Make it clear that they are not to include characters or action at this time. Get the children to read out their descriptions and vote on the best one. Try to get them to identify the reasons they preferred one to another.

Using old magazines, books, comics or postcards, cut out pictures of different locations. These can be mounted on a large sheet of paper to use as an ideas bank.

Get the children to paint or draw a setting for a story. They could use magazine cut-outs for some features, such as a yacht, a cliff, some trees, a planet in space, the interior of a space module or an ants' nest. They can write a short description of their own setting and these can be mounted along with the pictures.

Do a survey to find the top ten book titles in the class

and reproduce a description of the setting from each of these. Mount them together but on separate sheets, number them and leave the titles off. Over the course of a few days let the children read them to see if they can identify the books they came from.

Use **copymaster 83** (Settings) to encourage the children to think about the link between characters and settings. The first picture is of a setting with no characters, and the second of two characters with no setting. The children can work in pairs to discuss what they think is needed and then draw in the details. They can try to write a description of one of the settings.

Use **copymaster 84** (Ways to start a story) as an ideas bank for openings to a story. It can be reproduced at A5 size to fit into the back of an exercise book.

### Activity 6: Endings

Discuss some of the children's favourite stories with special reference to the way the action is resolved and how the story ends. Try to identify whether all the original characters are still in the action, whether the ending is satisfactory for them, whether it is happy or sad or even intriguing by leading onto another adventure. Try to think of examples of stories that end in different ways. What events contribute to the resolution of the story? Do they have elements in common like a strong character or superhero that sorts out the problems, a magical component such as the tools given by Aslan to the children in *The Lion, the Witch and the Wardrobe* or an element of good luck as in *Rumpelstiltskin*?

Discuss in detail one story that you have read recently to the class. All the children should be familiar with the plot. You can then discuss the following:

- what the main events were and how they lead to the final outcome
- how the characters behaved at the end
- whether the children expected this ending
- whether the children expected the characters to behave as they did at the end

- what the children thought of the ending
- how they think it could have been different.

Play a short game where the person who is 'on' has to give a simple outline of the end of a well-known story without mentioning the characters' names. The rest of the class or group have to guess what the story is. For example, 'This story ends when someone finds out the name of a little man, who stamps his foot so hard in his rage that he falls through the floor.' This is Rumpelstiltskin. You can be 'on' for the first few examples to show the children what to do.

Get the children to write short stories without the ending or reproduce some of their stories with the ending missed off. Next get the children to work in pairs with a story and think of a suitable ending. These can then be read out for you and the children to comment on.

Use **copymaster 85** (Ways to end a story) as an ideas bank for the final wording of stories.

Use **copymaster 86** (The reward) as an example of a short story for the children to finish off.

### Activity 7: Composing stories

By this stage the children should have written many stories but the work in this area of study is designed to help them think about and use detail beyond simple events. Try putting components together. Starting points are vital to motivation so as in Activity 5 where magazine pictures of settings were displayed to give the children ideas, get them to cut out pictures of characters too and display these alongside the settings. They can then pick a selection of settings and characters and build up events round them. Remind them to try to include short descriptions of settings, characters and the feelings of the characters at points of action in the story.

Use a storyboard for planning the outline and to jot down notes for descriptions and other details. Use **copymaster 87** (Storyboard) for this purpose.

 **NON-CHRONOLOGICAL WRITING**

Area of study 4

### Purpose

To encourage children to produce a range of types of non-chronological writing.

### Activity 1: Description of a person

There are many ways to describe a person. You can describe their physical attributes, their special abilities or their personalities. For a complete description, reference to all of these will be necessary. When describing their physical attributes the children will have to think in terms of how tall or heavy the person is; whether they have long or short hair; whether the hair is straight, curly or spiky; the colour of the hair, eyes and skin; whether they have any distinguishing marks or features, including a description of the way they walk, the way they talk and the type of clothes they wear. They

can then go on to a description of any particular skills or abilities the person possesses, for example, if they are particularly good at playing sport or a musical instrument, or if they are very skilled at drawing. Finally they can describe the personality of the person: how they interact with other people, whether they are happy and fun loving, shy and withdrawn, bossy and aggressive, or maybe a mixture of some or all of these. Encourage the children to write a description of one of their friends. Choose one person to read out his/her description and make sure they do not say the name of the person they are describing. The rest of the class or group are to try to guess who is being described and the first one to identify correctly gets the chance to read out their description next. Carry on until everyone has had a go. As the children get used to descriptive writing, they can be encouraged to include similes, to make their descriptions more interesting. 'Simile' comes from Latin and it means 'like' as in comparing one thing to another. A description of a person's features can be much more interesting if, for example, a person's eyes are not merely described as being 'big and round' but 'as big as saucers', or 'hair as spiky as a hedgehog's back'.

### Activity 2: Description of a place

When writing a description of a place for the purpose of providing clear detail, as opposed to setting a scene or an atmosphere, get the children to note precisely certain features of the place: light, time of day, weather, land use, vegetation, buildings and roads.

The idea is to draw a clear picture with words. Cut pictures of different places and locations from magazines and talk about the variety of features which are present. Then try to describe what the place looks like. When writing about a setting it is enough to mention one or two features such as 'The wind howled round the old empty house and the moon hid behind the gathering storm clouds.' But for a description of this kind we need much more detail, such as 'The old house was broken and empty. Tiles were hanging from its sloping roof and all the glass was gone from its huge ground-floor windows. The wooden steps leading up to the verandah were decayed and broken. The front door creaked as it moved to and fro in the howling wind.' Once again the use of similes in the description will enhance it and make it much more interesting. Once completed, the descriptions can also give the children further practice in recognising the differences between fact and opinion, and the children should be encouraged to look for those details which can be checked as measurements, for example, 'The house was about twelve metres tall' (a fact) and 'The house was the untidiest I ever saw' (an opinion).

### Activity 3: Plans and diagrams

Give the children plenty of opportunity to study plans and diagrams of all kinds, simple and difficult. Many of the good construction toys such as Brio Mech and Lego have diagrams for the children to follow. Get them to notice the use of language, which is instructional, directive and informative. The words are usually in the form of captions and labels. Give the children opportunities to write labels on simple plans and diagrams, and you can link this with other curriculum areas such as Science, Geography and History.

In Geography the children could be asked to write place names on a map, with reference to an atlas, or to look at the main geographical features of an area bounded by grid references. They can write street names onto a street plan of the local area, provided they have been given a reference point from which to start.

### Activity 4: Notes for Science or CDT

Both these subjects will need lists of materials and sometimes notes for hypothesis or a design brief. In CDT for example, the children may be asked to design something which performs a particular function. Get them to write notes on their drawing as they discuss their design, since these may be of use when it comes to the construction. These notes might be about how the axle fits on to a chassis of a vehicle they are making, or the notes might refer to the source of power for the vehicle and how it can be affixed to the body. Once they have started to build the model, get them to make notes about any problems they have encountered in the construction, and about the ways in which they overcame design problems due to the nature of the materials used.

In Science they can write about their hypothesis, and about how they set about testing it. They can record the equipment used and any interesting results they achieved. They can also include a diagram of the way

**Get the children to describe how they made equipment.**

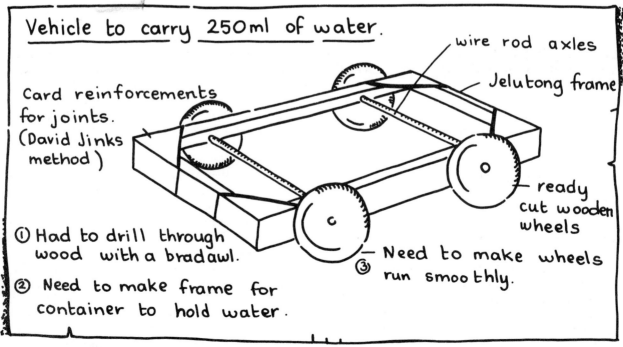

they set up the experiment and label it in the appropriate way.

## Activity 5: Making the rules for a game

Give the children an opportunity to devise their own games, either for playing on a board or in an open space. Form the children into small groups and discuss with them the sort of game they would like to create. Maybe it could be linked to a favourite television programme or to a particular sporting event, like the Olympic Games. The children have to think about how the players score, how they move about the board or open space, whether it is a team game and whether it is a game of knowledge or skill. You will need to identify the rules of familiar games to give the children some idea of the sort of thing that is required. This activity can be developed by allowing the children to make any equipment necessary, or to design the board in order to play their games and this will lead to much discussion and adaptation of the rules to make the game more enjoyable, interesting or easier to play.

## Copymasters

Use **copymaster 75** (Wanted) for the children to write a description of a friend, or of a desperate criminal. They can use the box for an illustration of their description, and write in the space below. This sheet can also be used for writing a description of the house of their dreams.

Use **copymaster 88** (Classified advertisements) for the children to write a description of a house, a musical instrument or any miscellaneous item that is for sale. For greater impact the children can look for pictures of houses or people in the Sunday colour supplements and these can be cut out and pasted onto the copymaster. The children can then use these for the purposes of descriptive writing.

Use **copymaster 89** (Captions) for the children to try and write suitable captions. The sheet can be used again by cutting photographs from a newspaper or magazine and the children have to try to think up a suitable caption to go with it. Discuss with the children the sort of things the characters in the illustration might be saying. The captions can be serious or amusing.

# REVISING AND REDRAFTING

Area of study 5

## Introduction

As teachers we are constantly assessing the writing of children. As a result many teachers see themselves as examiners in their response to children's writing. This role often increases as the child grows and many children become disheartened as their written offerings are reduced to mass of corrections in red ink. Many teachers link poor handwriting with little effort and reject tentative and hesitant work with the suggestion to try harder. The possibilities of turning such efforts into learning situations are therefore largely ignored. By encouraging the children to draft their writing as adults do, it gives them the chance to be free to explore the uses of the writing they have already acquired and helps them discover the limitations of rules governing it. The thing that children who are learning to write most need, is experience. This takes time. Helping the children to draft their written work and giving them a purpose for their writing helps them to use language to learn and, at the same time, gives them an opportunity to show what they have learned already.

## Purpose

To encourage the children to reflect upon what they have written, either with the teacher, another adult or with other children.

## Activity 1: Revision and drafting

When you first ask a child to write something, give them a piece of paper to make rough notes upon. This frees them from the restrictions of an exercise book where everything may need to be written very carefully and neatly. They can work alone or in groups but each child should produce their own first draft. When pupils present their first draft, it is important to show them

that we really are concerned with what they have written, that we think that what they have to say is important. With this first draft we have to forget for the moment such things as spelling, punctuation, grammar and handwriting. We must show interest and give immediate value to what the child has to say. We must emphasise what is good and try to encourage the child to think of ways of making what they have written even better. Make notes on their paper next to selected parts which are particularly good and also next to those parts which might need alteration to make them better. The child can then go away and reflect upon what they have written and, if necessary, make alterations. They may keep those parts they particularly like and rewrite or re-position other parts to improve it.

Independence can be encouraged by allowing the children to collaborate. Often a child will have little perception of whether a piece of writing is clear to another person. The writer should read through their own first draft and share it with a friend who can then respond to the writing and give advice to make it better. First of all the writer should, when they have finished writing, read it aloud to themselves and then ask themselves whether they are pleased with what they have written and whether there is anything they wish to change. Then they should read their writing to a friend and listen to their comments to see if they can think of any ways to improve it. Finally they should read or give their writing to an adult to read and see if they can offer any suggestions to make it even better. Those children who are responding to a piece of writing will need to listen carefully as the writer reads their work. Then they can say what they liked about the writing, whether anything is missing or anything is not clear or accurate, whether the beginning or ending is suitable and, if not, they can suggest a suitable one. Could some part of the writing be taken out? Will the intended audience understand the writing? Will they find it enjoyable and interesting? Is the writing of about the right length?

After this the listener may try to suggest some helpful words or expressions and then talk to the writer about suggested improvements. The writer can jot these down on a piece of paper, if necessary. By encouraging the children to write and discuss their writing with others it will help them to realise whether a piece of writing actually makes sense when someone else reads it. The relaxed atmosphere of working with another child can help the children to produce more detailed writing as the interaction promotes attention to detail.

Giving the children time and support in this way helps them to view writing as a shared activity and not something they have to produce entirely on their own. This builds confidence and encourages them to experiment in the knowledge that they will have an opportunity for reflection and redrafting so that having been jointly edited in a totally supportive way, which will include focusing attention on spelling, punctuation, grammar and handwriting at the various stages, their effort will be in a presentable state for the final draft. Thus they will have been involved in the finished work in a meaningful way and hopefully they will have learned a great deal in the process. As far as possible these principles and this approach should be carried over to all other types of writing in the curriculum.

# Attainment target 3: Writing

A growing ability to construct and convey meaning in written language matching style to audience and purpose.

| Level 4 | Statements of attainment | Example |
|---|---|---|
| | Pupils should be able to: | |
| | a) produce, independently, pieces of writing showing evidence of a developing ability to structure what is written in ways that make the meaning clear to the reader; demonstrate in their writing generally accurate use of sentence punctuation. | *Make use of titles, paragraphs or verses, capital letters, full stops, question marks and exclamation marks; set out and punctuate direct speech.* |
| | b) write stories which have an opening, a setting, characters, a series of events and a resolution and which engage the interest of the reader; produce other kinds of chronologically organised writing. | *Write, in addition to stories, instructions, accounts or explanations, perhaps of a scientific investigation.* |
| | c) organise non-chronological writing for different purposes in orderly ways. | *Record in writing an aspect of learning; present information and express feelings in forms such as letters, poems, invitations, posters, etc.* |
| | d) begin to use the structures of written Standard English and begin to use some sentence structures different from those of speech. | *Begin to use subordinate clauses and expanded noun phrases.* |
| | e) discuss the organisation of their own writing; revise and redraft the writing as appropriate, independently, in the light of that discussion. | *Talk about content and those features which ensure clarity for the reader.* |

# PUNCTUATION

## Purpose
To give the children further practice in using punctuation.

## Materials needed
An assortment of books and magazines, coloured pens, paper.

## Activity 1: Titles
Look at a collection of books and magazines to see how the titles are arranged in different places and for different purposes. For example, the front cover, the contents, the index, the preface and the chapter headings. Try to find examples of different lettering styles. Cut out story titles from magazines and comics and mount them as a collage to use as an ideas bank for styles. Encourage the children to observe that some titles are generally larger than others and discuss the possible reasons for this.

Give the children opportunities to practise organising titles for their own work. This can extend to other curricular areas such as making topic books, stories, reports for Science to be displayed near an experiment and instructions near apparatus such as computers etc. Let them use different lettering styles but draw their attention to the use of different styles and artwork to indicate content.

The punctuation conventions concerning titles are that a capital letter can be used for the first word only, or for all the important words but not for words like, 'and, of, at, to, a, in, on, for'. Titles are often written using all capital letters. When referring to titles in written material, they should be put within quotation marks like this: I read 'War and Peace' before tea.

## Activity 2: Paragraphs
Stories, accounts and other kinds of writing are usually organised into paragraphs because a long chunk of writing is difficult to read. Each paragraph is a set of sentences and deals with one main idea or topic. These topics could be the introduction of a new person, a new place, a change of time or a change of idea. The first sentence usually tells what the paragraph is about and is called the topic sentence. There is no rule about the number of sentences in a paragraph but the general idea is that there should be as many as is comfortable to read before having a slight break. When setting out paragraphs the convention is that each new paragraph starts on a new line and that the first word begins slightly further away from the margin i.e. it is indented.

a) Writing paragraphs. Give the children a small selection of topic sentences and ask them to write a paragraph about three of them. For example:
   1  It's good to have a friend.
   2  There is a park near where I live.
   3  I watched a good film last night.
   4  Our garden is full of flowers.
   5  My Dad loves fixing his car.
   6  I've got a bike.
   7  We went to the seaside for our holidays.
   8  Television is great.
   9  Sport is hard work.
   10  School can be good fun.

b) Let the children cut out three pictures from magazines or comics and then write a paragraph about each one. Remind them to start each paragraph with a good topic sentence.

c) Ask the children to think of two or more favourite things, activities or people and then to write a paragraph about each of them.

d) Using a picture as stimulus give the children three topic sentences relating to the different parts of a story and ask them to complete them. For example you may have a picture of someone holding a treasure map. The three topic sentences could be as follows:
   1  It was incredible to think that what Jim had found could be a real treasure map.
   2  He decided that the only thing to do was to go off in search of the treasure.
   3  There was the spot at last.
   The children can treat this exercise as an initial draft and expand the story later.

## Activity 3: Capital letters
At this stage the children should know already that capital letters are used to start a sentence and as the first letter of all proper nouns. They should also be used in the following ways:

- *as initials*. People's names, or part of them, are often written as initials. For example, Arthur George Bloggs can be A. G. Bloggs or A. G. B. A full

65

| | | |
|---|---|---|
| Fred Smith | F. Smith | F. S. |
| Jane Julia Topping | J. J. Topping | J. J. T. |
| John David Brown | J. D. Brown | J. D. B. |
| Alan Winstanley | A. Winstanley | A. W. |
| Mary Ellen Winters | M. E. Winters | M.E.W. |

stop is used after the initials. Get the children to write down the names of five people they know and the initials of those names, as shown above.

- *as abbreviations.* Some proper nouns can be shortened for convenience of writing. Many of these have been used for a long time and refer to people's occupations such as: Revd. (Reverend), Prof. (Professor), Capt. (Captain). These words can also be common nouns. The names of organisations can also be shortened in this way and this is increasingly the case these days. George Orwell was right in his futuristic vision of 'New Speak' in *1984*, as we now use 'Met' to mean Metropolitan Borough and abbreviate high street organisations such as Nat West and Nat Prov. The full stops are often left out as the abbreviation becomes more commonly used than the original word(s).

Ask the children to do a little research and compile two lists of abbreviated titles: the first of occupational or honorary names and the second of organisations. A dictionary and a telephone directory will be useful for this exercise.

The days of the week and the months of the year, which are also proper nouns, can be shortened in this way and should have a full stop after them. For example, Wed. 20th Sept.

Get the children to write out five or six dates of importance to their family or to themselves, using the abbreviated form.

My birthday — Wed. 12th Nov.

Mum's birthday – Sun. 16th June

Dad's birthday – Mon. 21st Feb.

holiday starts – Fri. 29th July

holiday ends – Sat. 6th Apr.

school trips – Thur. 10th Mar.

There are many other names of occupations, organisations and countries which are abbreviated by using the initials and a full stop, such as the following:

U.N. United Nations
B.B.C. British Broadcasting Corporation
U.S.A. United States of America.

Use **copymaster 90** (Capital letters) as an exercise in using capital letters in different situations.

### Activity 4: Full stops

This is the strongest punctuation mark and is used to show the end of a sentence. It is sometimes used in abbreviations and three full stops in a row indicates that some words have been left out. For example, when a sentence is left unfinished for dramatic effect then three full stops are used to show this: 'It was dark in the cave and . . . ' If part of a quotation is left out then three full stops mark the place: 'Said Simple Simon . . . indeed I have not any.' It is important to note that lists, labels and notices do not have a full stop.

Ask the children to think up five unfinished sentences which make the reader wonder what might happen next. They can be scary or merely interesting. Let them work in pairs so that they can discuss possibilities.

As part of some work for another area of the curriculum the children may need to design notices, labels and lists. To make the positive point about not using full stops you could have a lists challenge. Arrange a time limit and, letting the children work in pairs or small groups, ask them to make the longest list they can of any one of the following: towns in Britain, girls' names, capital cities of the world, countries, birds' names, makes of car, soft drinks etc.

The children should be able to think of many subjects. Let them use reference books or not depending on what skills you want to practise.

Use **copymaster 91** (Full stops) as an exercise in using full stops in different situations.

### Activity 5: Question marks

A question mark is used at the end of a sentence and is used instead of a full stop so the next sentence should start with a capital letter. A question can be just one word: Why? Who? When? How? What? When the words of the sentence are the actual question this is called a direct question and it expects an answer. When the sentence reports what question was asked it is called an

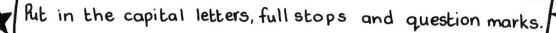

Put in the capital letters, full stops and question marks.

1. john jones was late for school

2. have you got your books

3. what time is it now

4. sue wanted to know what happened to tim

5. we are going on a trip on friday

6. he asked the way home

indirect question and does not have a question mark. For example, 'Where are you going?' is a direct question and, 'You were asked where you were going' is an indirect one. Short questioning clauses can be tagged on at the end of a sentence: 'It is late, isn't it?'

Give the children a collection of sentences, some of which are direct questions, some indirect questions and some simply sentences. Ask them to put question marks where necessary. You can leave out capital letters as well to make it a simple revision exercise.

Designing a poster for others is a taxing language exercise in that it must be written clearly with the intended audience in mind. Ask the children to design posters explaining the different punctuation rules such as use of capital letters and full stops or question marks.

Working together think of ten subjects which the children want to know more about and write them on the board. Next they have to pick one which appeals most and write down as many questions as they can about this subject. This can be extended into a research project by guiding the children to possible avenues of enquiry, such as the library, the museum, an organisation or a shop.

Play *Twenty Questions* and *Any Questions*. As suggested for Attainment Target 1 you can play these games but, to suit this purpose, write the questions down either beforehand or as the game proceeds.

Use **copymaster 92** (Questions) for similar exercises.

REMEMBER THE RULES O.K.?

1. Every sentence starts with a capital letter.

2. Every sentence ends with a full stop unless it is a question. Do you understand?

3. When we write lists we put a comma between each complete thing except the last two. These are joined by 'and'.
We had peas, chips, fish and jelly for tea.

## Activity 6: Exclamation marks

An exclamation mark is used at the end of a sentence or phrase to mark a special meaning such as joy, horror, anger, surprise, pain, danger or to attract attention when shouting. Too many exclamation marks should not be used in one piece of writing as it makes it difficult to read and the exclamation mark becomes less effective. Using more than one at a time is incorrect.

Use **copymaster 93** (Exclamation marks) to reinforce this work.

## Activity 7: Commas

Commas are one of the most commonly used punctuation marks and they can alter the meaning of a sentence. They are used to mark a slight pause, to make lists clear and to mark off words such as 'please, thanks, yes, no' when they have a meaning of their own. They are also used to mark off the name of someone who is being addressed. Commas are used in longer sentences which have two clauses, the comma coming before the conjunction. A subordinate clause is often separated from a main clause by a comma, especially if the subordinate clause comes before the main one. For example, 'When tea was ready, Mum called to the children.' Commas are not generally used before 'and' except where it helps to make the meaning completely clear. For example, 'The names of the flowers were Gemima, Sunburst, Perfection, Peaches and cream, and Beauty.' Without the comma after 'cream' we might think the last flower was called 'Cream and Beauty' or that there were six flowers.

As with other punctuation devices the children need opportunities to practise their use. Make and use worksheets, each designed to practise a different use of the comma and use a mixed sheet, like **copymaster 94**, for revision.

Use commas in composition. Give the children the opportunity to use commas in a set piece of writing, which can be fairly short, such as a letter, a descriptive passage, an account of an event or instructions, such as a recipe. You can get the children to write short plays, which obviously have a lot of dialogue and give the opportunity to use commas to mark off names.

Use **copymaster 94** (Commas) as a revision sheet or as basic practice in use of the comma.

## Activity 8 Punctuating speech

Direct speech, that is, the actual words someone says, is always written within inverted commas or quotation marks. Direct speech is set out in three ways:

- with the spoken words at the beginning of the sentence: 'I have made tea for both of you,' said Mum.
- with the spoken words at the end of the sentence: Mum said, 'I have made tea for both of you.'
- or with the spoken words at the beginning and the end, interrupted by the verb of saying and the subject speaking: 'I have made tea', said Mum, 'for both of you.'

Ask the children to think of a simple spoken sentence and a subject and then to write it in each of the three ways.

Capital letters are used to start the sentence whenever someone speaks but not, as in the example above, when the speech is interrupted.

When the spoken words come before the verb of saying they are followed by a comma outside the quotation marks if the quotation is continuous, as in the example above. If the quotation is broken at a point where it would naturally have punctuation, a comma should go inside the quotation marks, for example, 'My dear,' he said, 'I must go.'

When the spoken words are a question or an exclamation the punctuation for these is used instead of the comma inside the quotation marks: 'What's going on?' asked Dad.

When the verb of saying and the subject start the sentence a comma is used to punctuate before the quotation marks. For example: Mum replied, 'Nothing at all is happening, dear.'

Ask the children to think of five exclamations and five questions and to write them in a speech bubble as though they have been spoken by a cartoon character. They are to draw a suitable figure uttering each of these speeches. This work can be passed to a partner who then has to convert the cartoon speech into direct speech using the correct punctuation.

When writing conversations, a new paragraph should be started when one person stops speaking and another one starts. This means that the new speech should begin further in from the margin like a new paragraph.

"Red sky at night, shepherds' delight!"

Give the children the opportunity to practise this by providing them with conversations which are unpunctuated. The children could help to make a series of copymasters or workcards by copying out a passage of conversation from a favourite book and leaving it written as prose and not as direct speech. They could either write it by hand or type it on a word processor, depending on which skill you want them to practise. The writing can be mounted on card and given to another child to copy out correctly in the form of direct speech. The child making the card can make it more interesting by adding any illustrations or decorations they feel appropriate.

Where two sets of inverted commas are used in a sentence you can use single ones if a quote is given in direct speech so that there is less confusion. For example, use double ones for the outer marks and single ones for the inner. "I said to Jeff, 'What do you mean by that?' but he said nothing," moaned Elsie.

This work on speech can be extended by looking at the verb of saying. Ask the children to make a list of as many alternatives as possible to 'says' or 'said'. Write them in alphabetical order and display them as a vocabulary bank.

Use **copymaster 95** (Speech) to give the children practice in some aspects of this punctuation.

### Activity 9: Other uses of inverted commas
Foreign words, slang words, local words and specialist terms are often put in inverted commas to show that they are unusual. For example:
Cauliflower must be 'blanched' before freezing.
Mum felt 'drained' at the end of the day.

His Dad gave him a 'clout' round the ear.

See how many of these different categories the children know. Have a brainstorming session with you or some children writing the expressions you find on the board. You can have some children convert these lists into a poster for future reference.

Inverted commas can be used to show the reader that the author does not intend the literal meaning of a word and is being sarcastic, ironic or funny. For example: 'What a "delicious" meal of cold custard and chips!' laughed Tom with a grimace.

This time have a 'Funnies' sheet on the wall so that whenever the children come across such a usage they can write it down. You can look at them together after a period.

Inverted commas are used round direct quotations from books, traditional sayings or proverbs but do not need the commas used by direct speech. For example, 'Too many cooks spoil the broth.' Shakespeare and the staff room are usually a fruitful source of proverbs ancient and local! Children usually enjoy collecting and finding out about sayings and proverbs and may like to illustrate some of them in an amusing way. You can have them written out beautifully as a handwriting exercise, illustrated and mounted to be used in a 'Thought for the day' spot.

All titles of books, magazines, films, plays, TV programmes, songs, products and newspapers should go in inverted commas. Capital letters are used for the first word and any other important ones but not words like 'a, to, the, from, for' etc. Sometimes titles are written in capitals and in print they are usually printed in italic type.

# COMPOSITION

C96 –97

## Purpose
To give the children practice in writing stories and other chronologically organised writing.

## Materials needed
Usual classroom equipment.

## Activity 1: Types of writing
There are many different types of chronologically arranged writing and the children will be familiar by now with most of them. However, it is important to revise and collate knowledge acquired in diverse circumstances in order to make it meaningful for a particular purpose. Discuss the differences between chronological and non-chronological writing. You can also talk about the differences between real and make-believe stories and between fact and fiction. Draw up a discussion model on the board to show any features in common (see below).

See how many examples of such writing you can find around the classroom, that the children can think of or can bring in from home. Get them to make a display of different types of writing, using examples of their own work. They can produce their own labels and mount their own work at this stage. A diagram might help make the display more meaningful.

Writing that is organised chronologically includes stories, plays, narrative poetry, diaries, some newspaper and magazine articles, autobiographies, recipes, instructions of various kinds, reports of events and investigations in Maths or Science, comic strip cartoons, assemblies and other scripted performances such as video or audio taped programmes.

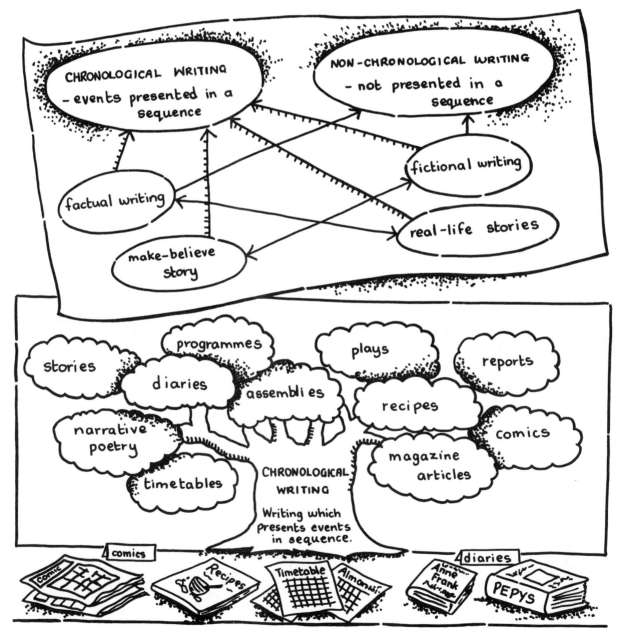

**Activity 2: Audience**

The Programme of Study for Key Stage 2 recommends that the children, 'should know for whom they are writing e.g. themselves (to help in their thinking, understanding or planning of an activity), their classmates, their teacher, younger children in school, their parents or other trusted adults.' Once this is known then the writing can be planned accordingly; the subject matter, style, length and vocabulary can be suited to the purpose. It is only when they start to write for other people that they realise, as the Programme of Study says '... writing for a public audience requires more care to be taken with the finished product than writing for oneself as an aid to memory.'

Ask the children to research the sort of audiences they might find for their writing, first of all in school and secondly outside school. Once they have discovered audience types then they can try to marry this with the sort of material the audience appreciates and their own writing repertoire. The first step would be to try to identify a need, for example, for news of school events or new stories to read. The reception or nursery class might not appreciate a highly technical report of a scientific investigation but they might enjoy short stories about little children at school or at home. The residents of an old people's home might like an amusing entertainment of the music hall variety.

Bearing in mind that this area of study is concerned with chronological writing, audiences and writing products could include the following:

a) within the classroom, for other children, the teacher or other adults: newspapers, reports (about work, trips, sporting events), class talks, stories, cartoon strip serials.

b) within school, for children of different ages, other teachers and adults, including parents: assemblies, plays, reports on events in different parts of the school, school magazines, stories for younger children, stories for children of different ethnic origins (either written in English at a suitable level or in the mother tongue with the aid of an adult translator and/or scribe).

c) within the local community, for adults and children of different ages: a local newspaper, local radio programmes about school or community events, guide booklets for places of local interest, local history stories.

d) in other schools, for children of different ages and teachers: stories for primary school children, stories about school events and traditions.

Use **copymaster 96** (Planning for the audience) to collate information about audiences in your survey. It can be used as a planning sheet for one selected audience. Block off the bottom half of the sheet before photocopying, then the children can use this section to plan their writing or make a rough draft.

In this area of study the instruction is that the children try to engage the interest of the reader. If they first research the tastes of the audience they can then look to the content of the writing.

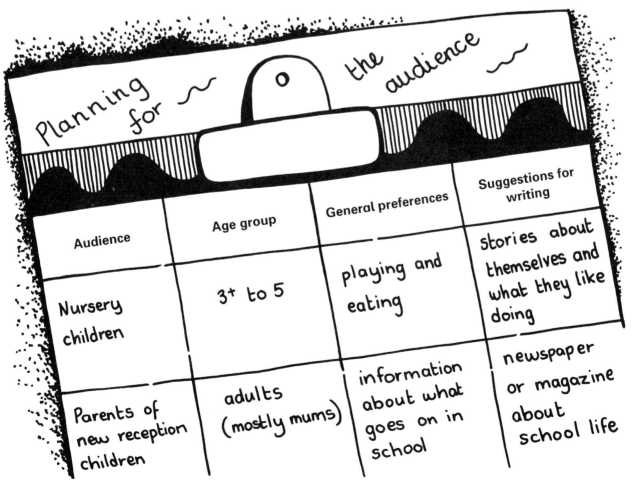

Planning for the audience

| Audience | Age group | General preferences | Suggestions for writing |
|---|---|---|---|
| Nursery children | 3+ to 5 | playing and eating | stories about themselves and what they like doing |
| Parents of new reception children | adults (mostly mums) | information about what goes on in school | newspaper or magazine about school life |

71

## Activity 3: Motivation and inspiration

Motivation or the reason for wanting to write is always important. As the children master the various writing skills the tasks become less daunting so that together with their involvement in the planning, they now have more control over their work and, hopefully, feel good about it as a result. Knowing and helping to select an audience are vital in continuing motivation.

Although inspiration and motivation sometimes come hand in hand, exactly what to write and how to start may elude the writer. As with the youngest children, private writing and writing about personal interests are a good source of inspiration for many types of chronological writing. For example, diaries, real stories about family or school holidays, accounts of personal investigations in Science or local history, personal accounts of school events like sports or performances are inspired by the child's involvement.

One good example of motivation and inspiration for private writing is used by the teacher of a Y6 class in Watermill Primary School. The children have this inside the cover of their private diary.

> This book is my space
> where I can write in my own way
> about what I learn in school.
>
> I write here for myself.
>
> I am not told what to write
> or when to write in this book,
> and I do not have to show it to anyone else
> unless I want to.
>
> No-one else can write in this book
> unless I invite them to.
>
> I can write about what I have enjoyed doing
> and learning about in school,
> and why it was good.
>
> I can write about what I have not enjoyed
> and why it was not so good.
>
> If I can't do something
> or if I don't understand something,
> I can try to work out why
> by writing about it for myself.
>
> I can write about things that happen,
> things we make, things we talk about,
> things I hear, things I read.
>
> I can write about what I think,
> what I feel, what I imagine.
>
> This book is for writing for me.

The Programme of Study says that the children should be encouraged to '. . . Write in response to a wide range of stimuli including stories, plays and poems they have read or heard, television programmes they have seen,

their own interests and experiences and the unfolding activities of the classroom.'

Seemingly ordinary things can provide the inspiration for stories, narrative poems, fact and fiction in the chronological form. People, places and things can produce, either on their own or in conjunction, both interesting starting points for stories or the inspiration for some factual research. Try some of the following:

- Bring in interesting objects, both old and modern, such as a jewel box, an old knife, a bottle, a candle snuffer, a tinder box, a map, a tea-towel, a note book, a dolly peg, a rubbing board, a ring, a shard of old pottery, a flint arrow head, a fossil.

- Bring in photographs of people, individuals and groups, old or new snaps. Put the real names of the people on the back, if known.
- Introduce two types of people from your current historical topic. Use a picture or a photograph of the people.
- Use photographs or write down the names of two to four people who are well known to the children. They can be known only to individuals or to the group as a whole. This could be a famous person such as a pop star. If the person is in school you could ask them to come into the classroom for a brief appearance/interview.
- Bring in an atlas, a map or a globe. These could be terrestrial, stellar, or oceanic. Also bring a collection of photographs of places such as cities, deserts, mountains, woodlands, cellars, the ocean floor, the earth from space, a front room etc.
- Have an inspirational cutting and sticking session. Get the children to cut out pictures from

**Story title: 'My island dream shattered.'**

magazines, old books or comics of people, places and things. Then let them choose the ingredients of their writing. This could be a selection of people, an object and a place. On the other hand it could be a picture of an object which could either inspire a narrative or start off some research into its manufacture. The children can mount their picture or picture collection and use it as inspiration for the planning stage.

- Tell of an exciting, ordinary or unusual happening at home.
- Speak about an interesting television programme.
- Watch a wildlife documentary video.
- Ask a visitor into school who has an unusual or an ordinary job.
- Bring in a pet, but remember DES regulations about animals in schools and make sure that the animal is properly supervised and handled.
- Bring in a baby or a toddler, or a small group of toddlers!
- Show a model which has been made or an experiment that is being run.

Also in the Blueprints series is *Writing*, a photocopiable book of inspirations for writing. Each page is a photocopiable sheet with a different idea and space for the children to write.

**Activity 4: Organising writing**

For fictional work, once the children have been inspired and have chosen or found a setting, characters and any objects which are material to the plot, then they can begin to organise their ideas about the action. They will need to plan an engaging opening, a series of events and then a resolution for the action and an ending. See pp. 57–61 for ideas which merely need the refinement of more practice at this level.

In the case of plays and other drama, the same planning details are needed as for a story but the way it is presented to the reader is different. Settings may be described in a few notes in the stage directions or they may be included or embellished within the dialogue, for example,

ANDY. It's certainly cold on top of this ridge, Jim.

JIM. It'll freeze by night-fall and the snow will be treacherous.

Characters are described by their actions and thoughts and by the other characters. They may also be described in the stage directions which may be fairly succinct as in Shakespeare's style, *'Enter: a crone.'*

Lined paper is useful when doing the first draft so that if the writing is double-spaced details can be added as the work is re-read. Play writing is a useful exercise in planning stories because the scene has to be set and the characters organised in writing, even in note form, before the action and the dialogue begin. For example,

*Scene: the battlefield*

*Characters: Henry IV, a servant.*

The children will find it useful to write stage directions in a coloured pencil or pen so that they can be spotted easily as children scan the page when reviewing.

73

A storyboard

| Characters | Place |
|---|---|
| Black Jake – pirate<br>Humbo – ship's mate<br>Crew of ship – some convicts, some<br>Customs men      press-ganged<br>Captain Hilton<br>His dog – Jem | cave – in cliffs – at sea level<br>high seas , spray<br>wind, rain |
| **Time** | **Main event** |
| night – moon full<br>winter | Customs men surprise pirates<br>fight<br>Black Jake's accident<br>dog discovers him<br>saved by customs men<br>pirates captured |
| **Opening**<br>title "Midnight raid"<br>pirates unloading brandy , seas high | **Ending**<br>Captain Hilton frees pirates |

There are several organisational devices to help with planning:

a) the storyboard. This is useful for fiction and nonfiction. The children can make notes in the various boxes and refer to them when doing the first draft of the story. It helps to think out the different aspects of the work in a model form, so that as it is planned, bits can be added or deleted according to the overview that the board allows.

Try analysing a story and converting it into note form on a storyboard to get an idea of how it works. Use **copymaster 87**.

b) the story map. This is a diagrammatic representation of a story which can take any form as long as it is clear to the writer what he or she intended. The writer should be able to explain the strategy to another person. Symbols and notes are used to represent the details such as setting, characters, sequence of events and endings. This is basically an analytical device but can be used to plan using a pencil and a rubber as the drawing unfolds flaws in the initial ideas.

c) the literary sociogram. This is a diagram which shows, using symbols and words, the relationships of the various characters in a story. This is also an

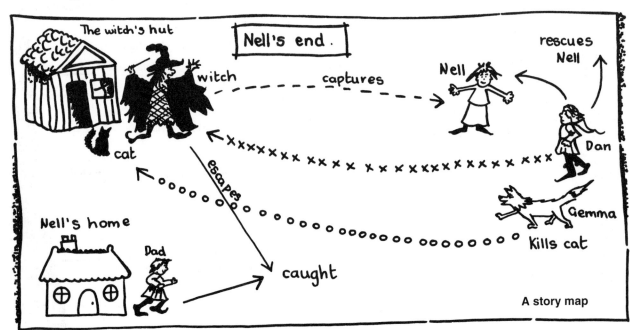

A story map

**A literary sociogram**

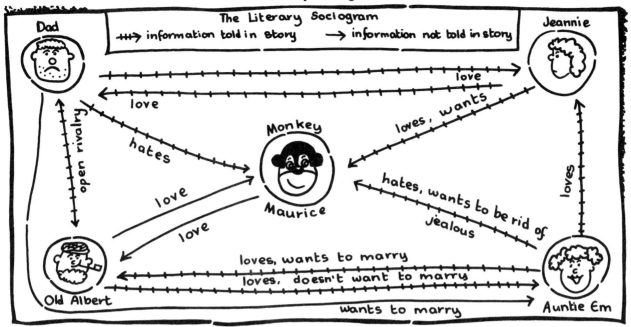

analytical device but can be used in the same way as the story map. In this case it can be used to work out complex relationships in a longer story.

In the case of factual stories or reports all aspects of the story and the chronology exist already, i.e. they do not have to be invented. A storyboard may be useful to recall all the elements of the happening or story and to put the events in order. Use a piece of lined paper to help with this. The children should initially try to recall the very first event and note it down near the top of the paper, leaving three to four lines empty so that if they remember something else as the planning progresses it can be written in above their first entry. Continue the

recall like this, leaving a few lines between each entry so that details can be added.

Planning chronological writing other than stories can be done in the same way, using lined paper to plan, for example, concert programmes, diaries of events, timetables, assemblies, topical radio programmes and any other writing which is organised chronologically. It is useful to start off with a piece of paper that has been drawn into several boxes so that the items can first be noted down as the children think of them then later organised into an order of events using the lined paper.

Use **copymaster 97** (Sequencing) as a planning sheet or as a blank for a cartoon story.

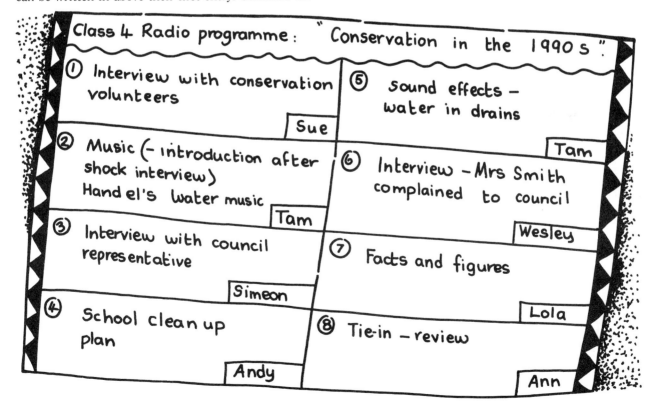

# NON-CHRONOLOGICAL WRITING

## Purpose
To give children practice in writing for different purposes in an orderly way.

## Activity 1: Writing about an aspect of learning
Ask the children to choose their favourite subject and try to get them to say why they like it and what it is about the subject that interests them. For example, if a child were to say that they liked Mathematics, they can try to list all of the aspects of that subject that combine to make it an enjoyable subject for them. The children can work alone or in small groups and they are to be prepared to present their findings to the rest of the class or to another group. Encourage them to think about such things as the kind of tasks they undertake which give them most pleasure: the practical aspect of Mathematics, the success they achieve, the recording or drawing of diagrams and graphs. It may be that they like the teacher or the method of teaching, the text books, workcards, working in groups or even being tested at various intervals. As an extension of this activity the children can then choose an aspect of learning that they do not particularly enjoy and do the same type of exercise to try and identify the aspects of that subject which make them feel that way. With careful handling the children can be organised into having a discussion based upon arguments for and against any aspect of learning in the curriculum.

## Activity 2: Presenting information
When information needs to be presented it should be done in an interesting way to catch the eye of the intended audience. The information may need to be presented in a variety of ways depending upon its nature. The simplest form is by way of signs. The signs can tell us what to do or they can warn us of hazards.

Give the children an opportunity to design a range of different signs that are either directional or prohibitive and these can form the basis of a display. Encourage the children to discuss the effectiveness, attractiveness and suitability of the different signs and see if the children can devise symbols which will get their message across without words, like traffic signs.

The next step is to devise posters which give information about an event. This may be an actual event which is to take place in school in the near future or it may be a poster to advertise a remarkable event in history. The children will need to make sure that they have all the relevant information such as dates, times and the people and places concerned. Then they are to present this in the most imaginative way possible. Once again this can make a most worthwhile class display.

## Activity 3: Writing a guide book
Encourage the children to write a guide book. This can be a guide book of the school or the local area. In each case the children will need to think carefully about the nature of the audience the guide is intended for. When writing a guide book about the school encourage the children to think about the kind of information to be included which will be of use to the reader. It might include: a short history of the school, a map showing the plan of the school area and classrooms, a list of the names of the headteacher and staff, a list of school governors, the name and address of the caretaker, short

paragraphs about out-of-school activities, clubs, societies and associations, a list of school holidays and any forthcoming events.

This list is only intended as a guide and the contents can be varied and placed in a different order as required. The children can be given a different section each and they have to try to present their information in the most interesting way possible. The culmination of their efforts can be the production of the guide for the use of visitors to the school, new pupils and prospective parents. The exercise can be repeated in the form of a guide book to the area in which the school is situated and the children can be involved in discussion as to what sort of useful information should be included to be of most use to the greatest number of people in the area.

## Activity 4: Writing letters

There are two kinds of letter. One is the informal letter we write to friends or relations. The other is the formal letter we write to people we do not know, or to businesses or organisations.

Show the children how to set out a letter. Show them how to set out the sender's address in the top right-hand corner, including the correct use of full stops and commas, put capital letters for the names of people and places, show them where to put the date and then talk about the way we can begin the letter. Talk about the words we can use, such as 'My dear . . .' or simply 'Dear . . .' followed by the name of the person to whom we are writing. Start off by doing this as group exercise, so that you can discuss with the children as you go along the points you wish to raise or emphasise. You can act as scribe to write out a letter to someone of the children's choice. Show them how to set out the contents of the letter in paragraphs, and then discuss the ways that the letter can be ended. As before you will have to discuss the variety of endings: 'Yours sincerely' or 'With best wishes', or indeed any appropriate ending to suit the content of the letter. Then give the children practice in setting out and writing a letter for themselves. They can write a reply to one of the following:

a) A friend, whose father is a famous record producer, writes to invite you to a special party where there are sure to be a number of pop stars. Write a letter accepting, and think of any questions you might like to ask at the same time.

b) A cousin writes to say that he is going away for six weeks and he has been trying to find someone to look after his pet crocodile. You are his last resort. What sort of letter would you write?

You can also talk about the postscript or PS and the position in which this normally appears. Give the children lots of practice in writing as many different kinds of letter as possible, including the more formal type of letter. Show the children how a formal letter is set out, with the name and address of the company or person to whom you are writing included on the left-hand side.

The formal letter might be addressed to a favourite television personality. The children will have fun composing such a letter and they can make their own suggestions as to the sorts of questions they wish to ask. The range of different types of letter is endless. They can be complimentary or critical of a particular programme on television like those read on *Points of View*. They can be thank you letters for a wonderful gift, letters asking for information about holidays, accommodation or theatre bookings, requests for payment, complaints about poor service and many other things.

The next stage is to give a sense of purpose to this activity by asking the children to write to someone of their choice: a famous person, a friend, the local authority, a politician, a relative or an organisation. Some national newspapers have a children's letters section and the children can be encouraged to write to one of these. The letters should be on a suitable subject for the person to whom they are addressed or should be written in response to a newspaper item. This will help the children to feel that their work has a real purpose, that it will be read, enjoyed and valued by someone other than the teacher. If you feel that you do not wish to get involved in writing letters of this sort, the next best thing is to try to liaise with a school in your area and exchange letters with them. The children can write to each other describing themselves, their hobbies and their interests.

Use **copymaster 98** (Letter) to give the children practice in setting out a letter. The subject of the letter can be varied to suit the occasion and the letters can be made more interesting by asking the children to imagine that they are, for example, a character from history writing to a contemporary about a great event. They might be a famous explorer describing their journey or the inventor of a really useful machine describing exactly how it works to a prospective manufacturer.

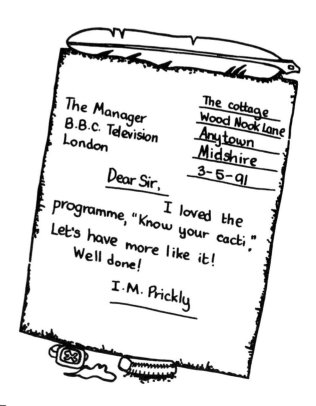

**Activity 5: Invitations**

As well as writing letters, the children can write out invitations. These can be purely functional, such as inviting parents to school to view a display or performance by the children. Alternatively, the invitations can be created to reflect an historical event or an idea from a book they have read. You will need to discuss the layout of the invitation and it might be a good idea to collect several types of invitation to show the children. They should all have received at some stage an invitation to one of their friend's parties or seen an invitation to a wedding. The children can then devise their own, incorporating a reply slip. At this point you can talk about the initials RSVP and what they mean or whether a simpler request for a reply to the invitation is more suitable.

Use **copymaster 99** (Invitation) for the children to write an invitation to a person of their choice. They can decide upon the type of event that they think the recipient would particularly enjoy. They could, for example, invite Nero to an exhibition of fire-fighting equipment, Henry VIII to a marriage guidance convention, or even 'Gazza' to a talk on overcoming shyness.

**Activity 6: Setting out poems**

Gather together anthologies which show the many different ways that poems can be set out and discuss these different ways with the children. Talk about the names given to the various types of poetry, such as limericks and acrostics. It is important to remember that children's poetry is often considered to be purely expressive and simply written emotion. Consequently the majority of it is not really poetic in the true sense of the word but more like an expression of consciousness which has been organised into lines. It has been shown however that children can benefit from more work on structuring this poetic expression and familiarisation

with these poetic techniques can heighten their expression. Acrostics are a very popular form of simple poetic expression. An example of such a poem written in this way is:

Sunshine reflected on the surface of the water,
Makes me think of happy days by the sea.
I remember the sounds and the sea breezes,
Lazy days lying on the beach.
Every time I think of these things I
SMILE.

Give the children a word like 'Smile' and ask them to write it vertically on a piece of paper. They can then start to try to write a set of sentences which begin with the initial letters. They can also try to see if they can connect the sentences in some way in order to create a more unified whole.

Limericks are another fun way of writing poetry. Give the children lots of examples such as:

There was a young lady from Lymm,
Who was so remarkably thin,
When she wore her best hat, which was quite round and flat,
she looked like a large drawing pin.

You can start the children off by asking them to complete the last line of a given limerick in their own way and then read them out to the rest of the group or class.

There once was a young lad called Ben
Who had a miraculous hen.
It would sit on the lawn, and with three bags of corn,

---

Encourage the children to look at the way poetry is structured and how the rhythm of the poem is determined by the use of words and the way the lines rhyme. Poems can have the first line rhyming with the second line and then the third line rhyming with the fourth, or the first line rhyming with the third line and the second line rhyming with the fourth. The rhyming word may come only at the end of the second line and the next rhyming word come only at the end of the fourth. Discuss all the different ways by looking at various anthologies and then ask the children to try to structure their poetry in a similar way. Encourage drafting, re-drafting and collaboration in order to give as much help as possible. Give a sense of purpose by making a book of poems to be read by other children or for a class display for parents.

Use **copymaster 100** (Poetry) as a sheet for the final draft of a poem on any subject. The sheets can be the pages of a book of poems, as suggested above.

# STRUCTURES OF ENGLISH

**Purpose**
To give the children practice in using different structures of written English.

**Materials needed**
General classroom materials.

**Activity 1: Sentences**
The children at this stage will be familiar already with the idea of simple sentences and should be competent using them. They can now begin to learn more about the structure of sentences in order to make their writing more effective and interesting.

The easiest way to present knowledge of this kind is by showing examples, asking the children to work on examples in a group situation with you and then to reinforce this learning by practising individually on worksheets. Real writing situations can then be used to apply the new knowledge and consolidate the concept. Naturally this new material should be presented in an interesting and visually attractive way.

What do they need to know about sentences? The children need to learn that a sentence is a group of words that make complete sense on their own.

*Simple sentences* have two parts: a subject and a predicate. The subject is the thing or person that the sentence is written about and the predicate is what is written or said about the subject. The verb is always found in the predicate.

*Example*
'Rocky loves mince pies.' is a sentence.
'Rocky' is the subject, 'loves mince pies' is the predicate.
The subject can be a group of words:
'Rocky the greedy parrot'.
If you ask yourself, 'who loves?' the answer is the subject: 'Rocky the greedy parrot'.

The subject of a sentence need not be at the beginning. It can be positioned in different places to make the reading more interesting.

*Example*
*The shiny green frog* leaped into the pond.
Into the pond leaped *the shiny green frog*.
Into the pond *the shiny green frog* leaped.

Simple sentences have different purposes. They can be statements, questions, commands, exclamations or greetings. In the case of greetings and commands the subject is often unstated as it is understood to be 'you'. For example, '(you) don't touch that!' or 'Happy birthday (you)!'

A simple sentence has one subject and one predicate. For example,
The witch/brewed a potion.
subject      predicate
However, the sentences can take the form of a question or a command.

Adjectives, adverbs and adverbial phrases can be added without changing it from a simple sentence

79

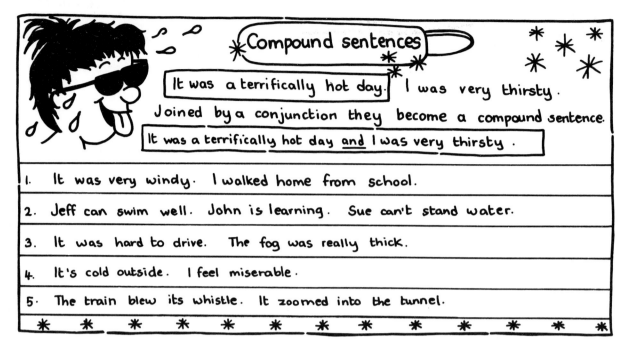

which still has only one subject and one verb. For example,

The wicked old witch brewed a potion.

adjective

The wicked old witch carefully brewed a potion.

adverb

The wicked old witch carefully brewed a potion/in her black cauldron.

adverbial phrase

*A compound sentence* is two simple sentences joined by a conjunction or separated by a comma, semi-colon or a colon. The separate parts of a compound sentence still make sense as each has a verb, a subject and a predicate.

Use **copymaster 101** (Sentences) to practise analysis of simple sentences. For compound sentences the example shown above is useful.

As a real writing exercise ask the children to take a short piece of their own writing and attempt to identify the simple sentences and then the subjects and predicates.

**Activity 2: Phrases**

A phrase is a group of words which does not make complete sense on its own and has not got a verb. If a subject and a verb are added to a phrase it can often be made into a sentence.

There are three types of phrases which can be added to a simple sentence to make writing more interesting: the adjectival phrase, the adverbial phrase and the noun phrase. They can be used instead of adjectives, nouns or adverbs.

*Adjectival phrases* describe nouns.

*Adverbial phrases* modify a verb by answering the questions: How? When? or Where?

*Noun phrases* describe a noun and can become the subject of a sentence like this:

All the children in school/enjoyed daily assembly.
noun phrase

**Activity 3: Clauses**

A clause is a group of words which are part of a sentence and contain a verb. There are two types of clause in a sentence and they are classified according to the job they do. The main clause is a complete sentence and can stand on its own, but the subordinate clause is dependent on the main clause for its meaning.

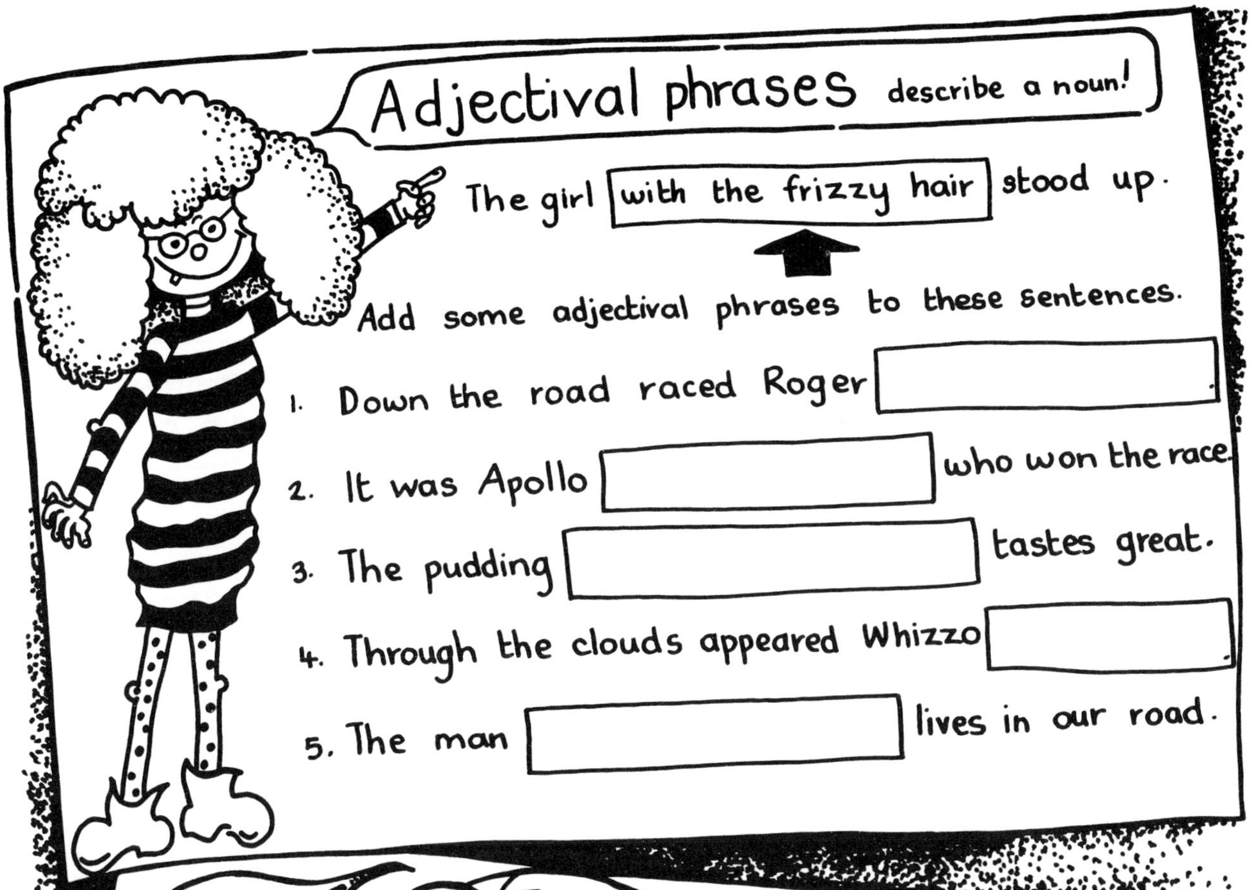

**Adjectival phrases** describe a noun!

The girl │with the frizzy hair│ stood up.

Add some adjectival phrases to these sentences.

1. Down the road raced Roger ☐

2. It was Apollo ☐ who won the race.

3. The pudding ☐ tastes great.

4. Through the clouds appeared Whizzo ☐

5. The man ☐ lives in our road.

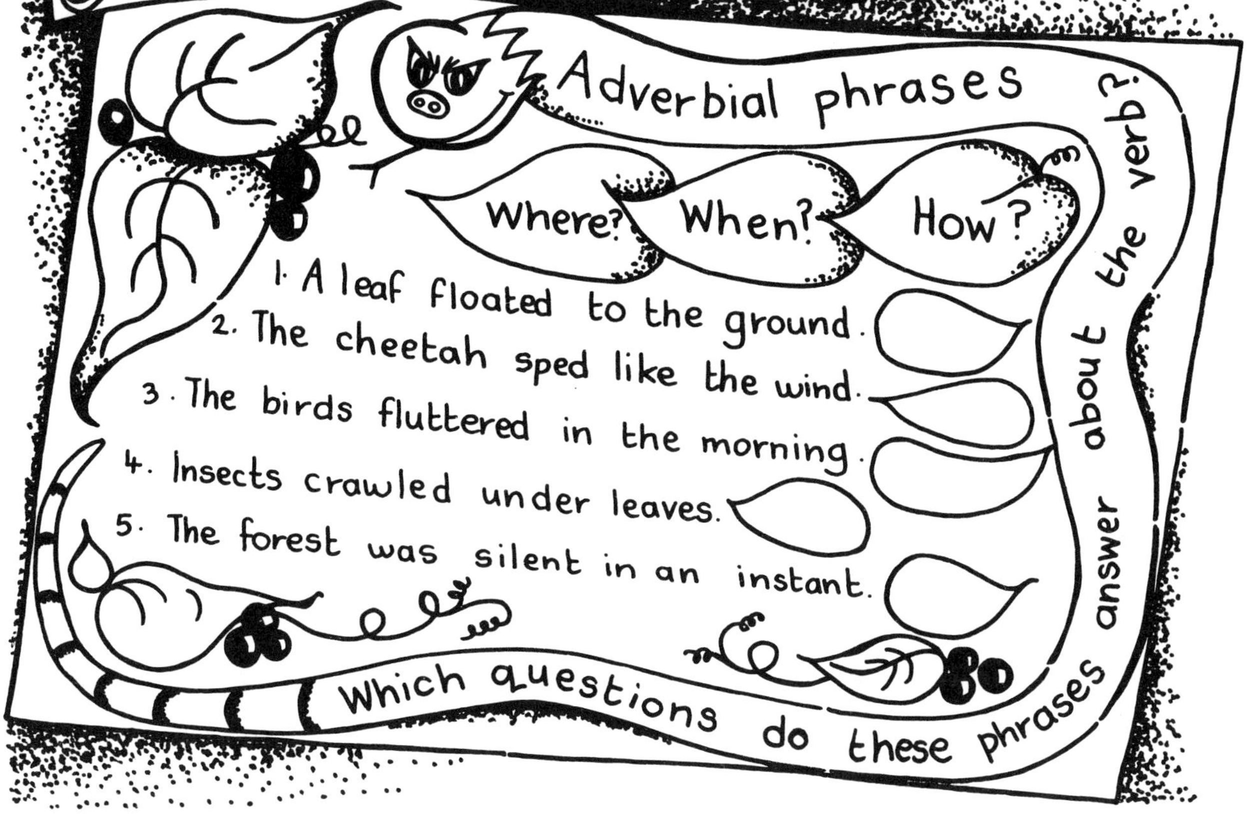

**Adverbial phrases**

Where?  When?  How?

answer about the verb?

1. A leaf floated to the ground.
2. The cheetah sped like the wind.
3. The birds fluttered in the morning.
4. Insects crawled under leaves.
5. The forest was silent in an instant.

Which questions do these phrases

For example,
Mum eats cream buns/when she is hungry.
Main clause          Subordinate clause

Clauses can also do the work of adjectives, adverbs and nouns and can help to make the writing more interesting to read.

The differences between the types of subordinate clause are quite difficult to understand and might be better left until Level 5.

*Adjectival clauses* describe a noun and often begin with 'who, which, that or whom'.

*Adverbial clauses* modify a verb and answer the questions: How? When? Where? or Why?

*Noun clauses* do the work of a noun and can be the subject or the object of the verb.

**Activity 4: Complex sentences**
A complex sentence is made up of a main clause with one or more subordinate clauses. These can be adjectival, adverbial or noun clauses. Subordinate clauses can be at the beginning or the end of a sentence and each clause contains a verb. For example,
When Sam got home,/she put on her track-suit/
adverbial clause          main clause
which was very comfortable.
adjectival clause

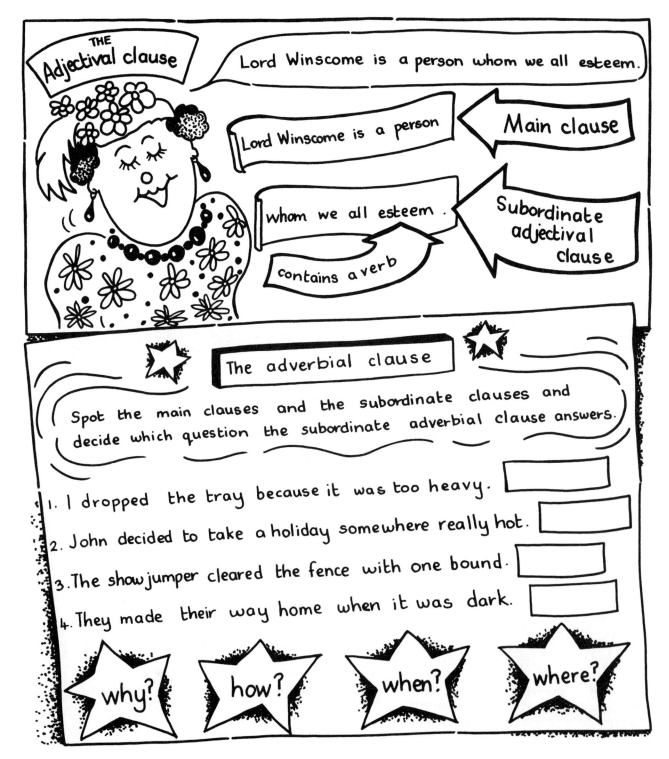

THE **Adjectival clause**

Lord Winscome is a person whom we all esteem.

Lord Winscome is a person

Main clause

whom we all esteem .

Subordinate adjectival clause

contains a verb

The adverbial clause

Spot the main clauses and the subordinate clauses and decide which question the subordinate adverbial clause answers.

1. I dropped the tray because it was too heavy.

2. John decided to take a holiday somewhere really hot.

3. The show jumper cleared the fence with one bound.

4. They made their way home when it was dark.

why?          how?          when?          where?

Noun clauses
Write a subordinate noun clause for these sentences. e.g.

Dad wanted to find out | what you have done.
← Here it is the subject. | → Here it is the object.

The rising of the sun | is wonderful to see.

1. Davy waited ages.

2. She ran down the road.

3. I began to think.

4. I want to see.

---

**REVISING AND REDRAFTING**

## Purpose

To give the pupils the opportunity to talk about, revise and reorganise their own writing, independently.

## Activity 1: Taking risks

On pp. 63–4 we set out a series of activities for the children to begin revising and redrafting their work in discussion with others. We showed that through discussion the children could be encouraged to think of ways to make their meaning clearer by collaborating with a friend to help with individual or joint writing tasks. As described earlier, teachers would respond first and foremost to the content of a piece of writing and then move on to its formal qualities. A suggested way of encouraging independent redrafting is to give the children an exercise book in which to write their first drafts. Encourage them to take risks and not to worry too much about the appearance or technical accuracy of the writing at this stage. Such features can be left till later when the writing is presented to an audience. They can leave line gaps between each line of writing so that they can be used for amendment or easy addition to the text, or alternatively use footnotes to make large scale alterations to the first draft. The children write their first draft and then read it to the rest of the class, a small

group or to one of their friends. After listening to the initial response they find out from their audience whether there is enough detail about what it is they are trying to say. They can make short notes at relevant parts of their first draft if they discover that there is insufficient detail about a particular aspect or if they have spent too much time describing another aspect. The amount of enthusiasm shown for particular parts of the draft will encourage the children to keep or discard them and will lead to the production of a revised draft. This too can be offered for consideration to the chosen audience and, as before, advice can be given for its improvement. The audience are to make suggestions in the light of what they wish to know or what they need in order to appreciate the writer's purpose in writing the text. Once the final stage has been reached the final draft can be written. At this point careful consideration can be given to presentation and spelling. The final draft can be written on a computer or word processor if desired and use can be made of the spell check facility. Revising and redrafting in this way can encourage the children to begin to apply the range of critical skills in listening to or reading each other's writing that is usually reserved for published books. In this way, a very constructive writing atmosphere can be achieved.

# Attainment target 3: Writing

A growing ability to construct and convey meaning in written language matching style to audience and purpose.

| Level 5 | Statements of attainment | Example |
|---|---|---|

**Pupils should be able to:**

a) write in a variety of forms for a range of purposes and audiences, in ways which attempt to engage the interest of the reader.

b) produce, independently, pieces of writing in which the meaning is made clear to the reader and in which organisational devices and sentence punctuation, including commas and the setting out of direct speech, are generally accurately used.

c) demonstrate increased effectiveness in the use of Standard English (except in contexts where non-standard forms are needed for literary purposes) and show an increased differentiation between speech and writing.

d) assemble ideas on paper or on a VDU, individually or in written discussion with others, and show evidence of an ability to produce a draft from them and then to revise and redraft as necessary.

e) show in discussion the ability to recognise variations in vocabulary according to purpose, topic and audience and whether language is spoken or written, and use them appropriately in their writing.

**Example**

*Write notes, letters, instructions, stories and poems in order to plan, inform, explain, entertain and express attitudes or emotions.*

*Make use of layout, headings, paragraphs and verse structure; make use of the comma.*

*Understand that non-standard forms for literary purposes might be required in dialogue, in a story or playscript; use constructions which reduce repetition.*

*Draft a story, a script, a poem, a description or a report.*

*Discuss the use of slang in dialogue and narrative in a published text and in their own writing and comment on its appropriateness.*

---

**Area of study 1**

# VARIETY OF FORM AND PURPOSE

**Purpose**
To give the children opportunity to write for a range of purposes and audiences.

**Materials needed**
General classroom materials.

**Activity 1: Thinking about audiences**
By now the children should have had some experience of writing for different audiences but, as they work towards Level 5, they should be able to more accurately question the purpose of their writing and be able to plan it more effectively. They should now begin to realise the power of their writing as effective communication by asking themselves questions, such as: Who is my audience? What does my audience need to know? What message do I want to put across? How can I do this? What does my audience like or relate to? What effect will my writing have on the audience?

Plan small research projects to find out what types of writing suit different audiences. Try to establish very simple but specific research questions. For example: Can the reception children understand directional notices with lots of writing? What level of writing do the reception children understand? What type of stories do the lower juniors enjoy? What do parents want to know about school life?

Research techniques at this level could include surveys, interviews and questionnaires. Encourage collaboration by getting the children to work in groups.

84

## Activity 2: Thinking about purposes

Discuss the idea of writing being a form of communication. This could be part of a wider topic on communication. The idea of writing is that it engages the interest of the reader in some way. Try to find examples of writing which informs, directs, entertains, warns, organises, greets, pleads, persuades, comforts etc. Ask the children to make a display of the purposes of writing, using examples they have produced themselves. You can organise them into groups and give each one a different type of writing to illustrate.

## Activity 3: Types of writing

Writing for a real purpose is most important but at this stage writing for an imaginary purpose can also be entertaining and fruitful. Different types of writing suit different purposes and for real situations they include:

letters to pen friends at other schools, home and abroad;
letters to firms and organisations as part of topics;
letters to parents about school events;
plans for trips and projects;
class and school timetables, for lessons, tuck shops, library use and clubs;
instructions for use of equipment or facilities;
instructions about behaviour in certain circumstances e.g. fire drill;
posters advertising school events;
merit awards;
directional posters;
a personal diary for private use only;
stories for other children (peers and younger age groups);
greetings cards and messages;
plans and diagrams.

Types of writing for imaginary purposes include:
letters to story characters;
the diary of an established character or a character of the writer's own invention;
greetings cards for imaginary characters, such as a birthday card for the BFG or a wedding invitation from Cinderella.

### Activity 4: Planning the writing

Once the audience, purpose and types of writing have been established, the finer planning details have to be worked out. Think about the following:

* language to suit the ability and interests of the reader
* print: size, style, colour, use of capitals or lower case letters
* illustrations: colour, style, position, quantity, subjects
* format: general appearance and layout

See pp. 70–5 for ideas on organising the writing.

## ORGANISATIONAL DEVICES

Area of study 2

C102 –103

### Purpose

To show the children the correct use of layout, headings, paragraphs, verse structure and the setting out of direct speech.

### Activity 1: Correct use of layout

When writing a piece of text the layout is very important as this can help the reader to make sense of what it is we are trying to say. This is particularly important when writing notes for a Science experiment, or writing about a CDT project or a cookery lesson. In order to give the children some idea of the variety of ways a text can be set out, collect some newspapers, magazines, comics and books, and ask the children to look at them carefully. Point out the use of bold print for headings, the imaginative use of illustrations (see page 87) and photographs, the use of sub-headings, captions and paragraphs. All of these organisational devices help the reader to understand the text more easily and also enable them to identify the different parts of a text, especially when it refers to an activity. The planning of a piece of writing makes the task that much easier. Short compositions can be planned in a number of paragraphs, and planning paragraphs can be done by making notes and then placing the notes in a sensible order.

The first step is to ask the children to make notes about a particular topic. Some of the notes will come from what they already know. Others will have to come from books. At this stage they can be in any order. The next step is to make an outline. This means arranging the notes in a sensible order and when they do this they must remember that the first sentence of the paragraph must tell the reader what the paragraph is all about. The second thing to remember is that the sentences in the paragraph must lead smoothly from one fact to another. When the children are looking for information in books point out the value of the organisational devices in helping them to identify the parts of the book where the information they seek is likely to be found. They can then try to incorporate them into their own accounts. Encourage the imaginative use of bold letters or type for titles and paragraph headings. Talk about the position of the text in relation to the position of the illustrations.

If the children are writing up notes for a Science experiment, their first task is to plan their work in sections. First of all they think about the different aspects of the experiment and jot down possible headings. The title could be the name of the experiment, such as 'Why do things float?' Next they must write down their sub-headings. The first paragraph will be about what they were trying to find out and why they were conducting the experiment. The first sub-heading can then be 'Equipment used' with a short list of the items they needed for the experiment. They can then write a paragraph about any hypothesis and say how they used the equipment to test this. Next will be a paragraph on what they discovered using the equipment and they can also try to give reasoned explanations to support their findings. Finally their last paragraph might include a report on testing a set of variables in order to ensure a fair test.

If you look around you can see things that work like bridges, but do not look like them.

If the children are writing stories for younger people let them look at books written for that age group, so that they get some idea of the types of layout. By placing the illustrations in unusual places they can add an extra element of enjoyment for their audience. They might also think of variations to the lift-the-flap books, pop-up books and the revolving wheels incorporated into many illustrations. This activity also has implications for CDT where the children can actually produce a design brief, see the design through to its finished state, and test it by reading the book to a group of younger children to gauge their responses.

### Activity 2: Verse structure in poetry

Following on from the work done on p. 78, the children will have had lots of experience of the many different ways in which verse structure influences the layout of poetry. The meter or the rhythm of the poem determines the length of the line and the incidence of rhyming words often determines the length of the verse, if indeed the poem is written in verses. By giving the children plenty of opportunities to look at and read poetry they will become familiar with the layout and the possibilities of verse structure and they can be

encouraged to attempt their own. It may be possible to give them some instruction in the use of a thesaurus at this stage in order to help them to search for alternative words that will make their poem rhyme.

All of these activities can be used in the creation of the class newspaper. The skills of layout can be further utilised in making-up the pages in order to create an attractive newspaper. By arranging the articles on a large sheet and providing suitable illustrations to accompany them where necessary, the children will be able to make value judgements as to the effectiveness of layout based upon their own requirements.

### Copymasters

Use **copymaster 102** (Layout). The children read the text and set it out in paragraphs, adding suitable headings and sub-headings, and putting in quotation marks and other punctuation where necessary. The two poems can be photocopied separately at the top of a page to leave space below for children's work.

Use **copymaster 103** (Verses). The children read the poems as written on the sheet and then try to arrange them according to their interpretation of the verse structure.

 **STANDARD AND NON-STANDARD FORMS**

Area of study 3

### Introduction

The Programmes of Study for Key Stage 2 state that, 'in order to achieve Level 4 children should be able to recognise the grammar and vocabulary differences between Standard English and the local dialect of English.' To achieve Level 5, 'Pupils should be helped to extend their range of vocabulary and increase their awareness of what is suitable according to purpose and context.' So, at this level children need opportunities to use both Standard and non-standard English.

### Purpose

To give the children opportunity to use both forms of written English.

### Materials needed

General classroom materials.

### Activity 1: Using Standard English

The Programme of Study further states that, 'They should have opportunities to write for formal and public purposes so that there is valid reason to use Standard English in their writing.' Writing of this kind could include:

- letters – of enquiry, request, thanks and complaint. These could be to firms or organisations as part of work in other curricular areas, to places which have been visited, or to speakers or groups who have

visited school. Letters to parents from school could also be written.

- notices – of the more formal kind, such as instructions about first aid or fire drill, or behaviour in work places like the library and information about formal school meetings.
- reports – about work, projects, events, trips, which are to be read by parents and other adults in a formal setting, possibly the school magazine.
- invitations – to parents and other community members to school functions.
- instruction manuals – about school equipment which children use.
- anthologies – of poems and stories for peers and younger children.
- stories – for younger children in school and at local playgroups and nurseries.
- a school radio programme (on audio tape) which includes reports of a formal or serious nature or school news bulletins. Items such as this can also be delivered in dialect or using the current media slang both of which are non-standard English.

Scripts would need to be written for these performances. Listen to radio and television news for examples of news delivery in Standard English.

- forms and questionnaires – such as those used by clubs for membership applications, swimming lessons, reserving a library book or for conducting surveys.

At this level the children should be helped to widen their formal vocabulary in each of the situations described above. For example, words like, 'pleased, grateful, helpful, sincerely, appreciate' might be used in a letter of enquiry. Talk about the vocabulary which is suitable before starting work.

### Activity 2: Using non-standard English

Some of the situations given above might also be suitable ones in which non-standard forms can be used, depending on the occasion and the audience. For example:

- anthologies – of poems and stories, could use dialect in prose or speech.

- stories – for younger children could use dialect or colloquialisms in the story form or in direct speech.
- school magazine – could use dialect, slang forms in reports, articles, notices, advertisements and titles. For example, 'Crucial reading'.
- school radio programmes – could use the type of disc jockey banter as used on real pop programmes.
- dramas – dialogue in plays may be written in non-standard forms except, of course, if a formal situation is being portrayed such as a coronation, an arrest or a court scene.
- notices – at informal occasions like parties or clubs.

### Activity 3: Research
Set up a short research project to find out where both forms of English are used. Ask the children to find as many examples of both forms of written English as they can, in school, at home, or in the wider community. Ask them to discover which types of writing can use each form of English and which use both.

### Copymasters
Use **copymaster 104** (Research into writing use) for collecting information for the above project.

| Type of writing | SE/NSE | Purpose of writing | Place used |
|---|---|---|---|
| letter | SE | from school to parents about parents' evening | school and home |
| instruction book | SE | to show children how to use new computer | school |
| diary | NSE | for writer's own interest and record | home |

## DRAFTING AND REDRAFTING
Area of study 4

### Purpose
To give the children further opportunities for drafting and redrafting.

### Activity 1: Assembling ideas on paper or VDU
Following on from the activities on pp. 63 and 83 the children will have had plenty of opportunities for revising and redrafting. Give them further opportunities and encourage them to write a composition in the following way. The first step is to think about the topic they wish to write about and make brief notes of their thoughts as they occur, jot them down on paper or on a VDU. If they do not know enough about the topic already then they will need to look up some facts in books of information or from any suitable source. If they are writing a story, a script, a poem, a description or a report, their notes may take a different form to those of a topic. Once they have written their notes they will have to start to organise them in a suitable way, making use of the skills learned at previous levels and in different attainment targets. Their success at this task will provide suitable evidence of their ability to revise and redraft at this level.

There are many programs available which allow the children to assemble their ideas on VDU. Advance Folio from ESM is a very good package which helps the children to develop punctuation skills and understanding of sentence and story structure for work at Levels 2 and 3. With the word processor, it is ideal for revising and redrafting work, for use with BBC B, B+, Master 128 and Master Compact. Junior Desktop is a fully integrated package for the BBC Micro. This is a word processor, a database, a spreadsheet and a graphics package all in one and all capable of sharing the same data. Each program can be used separately or together to cover many aspects of the curriculum and many forms of presentation. Children can write a description and print a report of their work with graphics included in the text. This package covers many IT tasks in the National Curriculum and, used with a spell checker, will help the children come to terms with the requirements of this level of this attainment target. The range of software packages is constantly being improved and updated. A good source of information for such programs which is regularly updated and revised is the AVP Guide to computer software for primary schools available from: AVP, School Hill Centre, Chepstow, Gwent, NP6 5PH.

This gives a very extensive range of software for all areas of the curriculum, for use with BBC, RM Nimbus, IBM PC and Archimedes.

# VARIATIONS IN VOCABULARY

**Purpose**

To give pupils an opportunity to discuss variations in vocabulary and comment on the appropriateness of it in the given situation.

**Activity 1: Recognising the variations in vocabulary**

There are many occasions when the vocabulary used in dialogue or in a text is different to the so-called Standard English that most of us use. Discuss with the children the occasions when words are used which may not be familiar to them or not even used in everyday speech. Collect together some specialist magazines about such things as computers, medicine, antiques, car repairs, knitting and as many others as you can think of and talk about the people who might buy them and whether they would need some knowledge of the subject before they could understand the technical terms in the text. In all these instances the magazine is aimed at a particular audience: those people who already have some knowledge.

Ask the children whether there have been any occasions when they have been watching a film or listening to a record and they have not understood the meaning of a word or phrase. You can now begin to talk about the use of slang, colloquialisms and dialect in dialogue or narrative and the suitability of its use. A colloquialism is an expression used in ordinary conversation but not regarded as slang, for example 'feeling under the weather' or 'three sheets to the wind'. The first expression refers to someone who is feeling unwell and the second is describing someone who does not quite know what they are doing or who has no sense of purpose. Both of these would be quite at home in a soap opera and sometimes writers use such phrases to heighten the sense of atmosphere and location in their stories. Similarly, writers often use slang and dialect in order to convey a sense of realism in their stories. Slang is a word or expression in common colloquial use but which is not regarded as Standard English and in some places is not acceptable at all. Writers trying to create a sense of realism would try to give their characters the right sort of vocabulary in order to achieve this. In a book about gang rivalry among youngsters on an inner-city council estate, it would be no use using vocabulary more commonly associated with a set of children from a rich middle-class area. Ask the children to go to the library, look through a suitable range of fiction and try to identify any parts which contain slang or colloquialisms, then discuss their suitability in context. Make recordings of television programmes set in different locations and try to identify colloquialisms and slang. Dialect may be more easy to identify, depending upon the area where the programme is set. The sound of the voice and the inflection on different words, especially with strong local accents, can give a clue as to the location of a particular dialect but this may not be enough to help with the understanding of the text or narrative. A useful way of discussing local dialect is to invite people who still retain their dialect to come into school and talk to the children. This will have even greater meaning for them since they will be able to see it in use. Collections of poetry and songs in local dialect are always interesting and provide really practical examples for the children to try and interpret.

Ask the children to try to identify occasions when a different type of vocabulary might be necessary in everyday life. Radio communication has a language all of its own. People such as police officers, ambulance personnel and taxi drivers use their own call signs when communicating with their headquarters and they may have special phrases which they use in order to pass information secretly. Similarly with aircraft pilots and air-traffic controllers, the vocabulary they use is very specialised and we would find it difficult to understand.

**Activity 2: Using the variations in vocabulary in writing**

After much discussion and identification of the many variations in vocabulary according to purpose, topic and audience, ask the children to choose a situation where they might have to acquire some specialist knowledge about a given subject or topic in order to include suitable vocabulary in a piece of text. Such situations might be:

- a pilot radioing the air-traffic controller for directions for landing
- a doctor describing in medical detail the injury resulting from a broken leg and how to treat it
- a quarrel between two people from the East End of London or from any large city near your school
- a discussion between two stockbrokers about their day in the City.

Each of these pieces of writing will involve the children in finding out for themselves the sort of terms, language and phrases used by the different sets of people.

**Copymasters**

Use **copymaster 105** (I see what you mean) for the children to identify which group of people in the illustrations said which set of words.

# ATTAINMENT TARGET 4: Spelling

## Attainment target 4: Spelling

| Level 3 | Statements of attainment | Example |
|---|---|---|
| | Pupils should be able to: | |
| | a) spell correctly, in the course of their own writing, simple polysyllabic words they use regularly which observe common patterns. | *because after open teacher animal together* |
| | b) recognise and use correctly regular patterns for vowel sounds and common letter strings. | *-ing -ion -ous* |
| | c) show a growing awareness of word families and their relationships. | *grow growth growing grown grew* |
| | d) in revising and redrafting their writing, begin to check the accuracy of their spelling. | *Use a simple dictionary, word book, spell checker, or other classroom resources; make spelling books or picture books.* |

 **Area of study 1** | **A STRATEGY FOR COMMON PATTERNS** | C106 –107

### Introduction

The range of sound patterns covered in Key Stage 1 level 2 is extensive and covers most of the words children regularly use at this level too. We recommend that these same sounds are reinforced at this level so that, in conjunction with the following areas of study, a wide body of knowledge is established.

The following sound patterns were introduced in Level 2: th, sh, ch, ea (two sounds), oi, oy, ai, ay, ow, ou, oa, fl, cr, dr, bl, st, sk, nt, nd, ff, ss, qu, ph, kn, magic e and the vowels. These sound patterns could be introduced at this level: er, or, ew, ur, ar, aw, au, mb, wr.

Straightforward facts are difficult to absorb so it is best to vary the approach and to refer the knowledge learned to its practical application in the children's own writing. A lively class brainstorming session is a good way to introduce sounds and a large cut-out or drawn sound is a good visual focus.

The children will be able to contribute many examples of words containing the sound and these can be added to a giant list of words. Leave this on display for a week so that they can add to it if they come across further examples in their work.

We will not cover the full range of common spelling patterns in this area of study but will use some of them

as examples. The following activities will be useful for several purposes: to introduce the sound, to show how it is used or as reinforcement. However, it is vital that you take the opportunity to point out examples of words using the sound in any other curricular areas, particularly in the children's own writing. The general strategy should be to identify the new sound, find examples of its use, use it and make a conscious attempt to remember it.

**Purpose**
To help the children to spell regularly used words which observe common patterns.

**Materials needed**
General classroom materials, card, glue, scissors, Sellotape.

**Activity 1: Word grid**
Using any new sounds that you have introduced, make a word grid as shown above. Put in eight to ten words which contain the new sound so that the children can search for these words.

**Activity 2: Search in context**
Write a short passage or a set of sentences which contain words using the new sound and ask the children to read this and underline the words containing the new sound (see top of opposite page). An amusing passage is always more interesting. When designing such work, you will first need a list of as many words as possible containing the new sound, so that you have a good selection to choose from when composing the passage. You can make this list with the children when you introduce the sound.

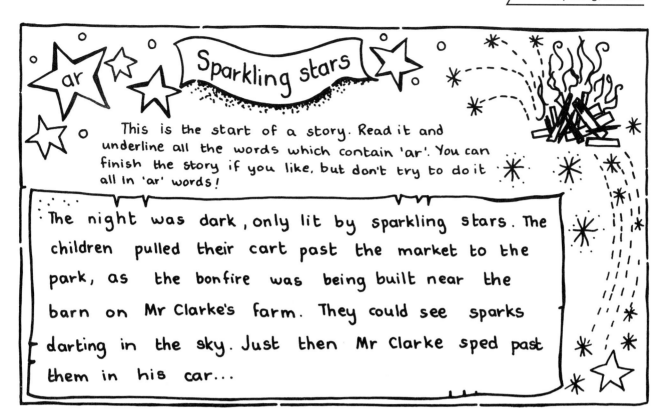

**Sparkling stars**

This is the start of a story. Read it and underline all the words which contain 'ar'. You can finish the story if you like, but don't try to do it all in 'ar' words!

The night was dark, only lit by sparkling stars. The children pulled their cart past the market to the park, as the bonfire was being built near the barn on Mr Clarke's farm. They could see sparks darting in the sky. Just then Mr Clarke sped past them in his car...

### Activity 3: Complete a word

Using about ten words containing the new sound write them down with the new sound omitted and ask the children to fill in the missing sound to complete the words. Write each word within a shape of its own or in a large shape which is related to the meaning of one of the words. For example, if the new sound is 'ar' draw their sound inside a shark and write the words to be completed inside little fishes being chased by the shark. Another example is shown below for 'ur'.

### Activity 4: Sort into sets

Introduce two new simple sounds at once and reinforce both by mixing up words containing both sounds. Ask the children to sort them into two sets in a simple exercise as shown overleaf.

### Activity 5: Dictionary search competition

Using a simple children's dictionary ask the children to search for as many words as possible which use a particular new sound. Get them to work in pairs and make it into a competition by setting a time limit and possibly having some kind of award for those who find the most words. Pool the words the children find and compile a giant list for the classroom display.

### Activity 6: Snap

Get the children to help make snap cards. Use sounds you have already learnt so that this is a revision exercise. You can use just sounds or words containing the sounds. Make three or four examples of each item to give adequate opportunity for 'snap' and use about ten items. Get the children to write them using brightly-coloured felt pens.

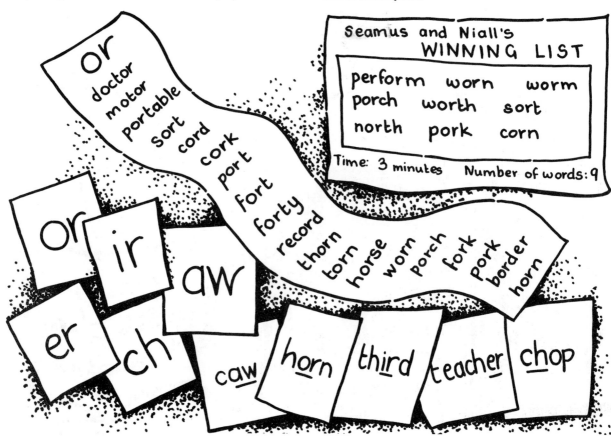

### Activity 7: Lotto

Get the children to help you make a lotto game using either words which use the same sound pattern (to introduce it) or a selection of words using different sound patterns (to consolidate a section of learning). Organise them into small groups to make the game and then let that group play together. Ask the children to illustrate the cards with patterns or pictures, if appropriate. They can also think up a name for the game and store it in a decorated box or folder, suitably named.

### Activity 8: Pairs

Using paper or card, playing-card size, the children should work in pairs and write out ten words from each of two sounds. They should do this twice so that you have a collection of forty words. Use four different coloured felt pens to write the words so that, for example, you have ten words containing 'ew' written once in red and once in blue, and ten 'ow' words written once in yellow and once in green. Make the cards into a pack and shuffle them well. Now the pair of children can play a type of solitaire. They take half the pack each and, taking turns, place the cards on the table in sets of sounds and colour, matching the words as they go. The aim is to match up all the pairs. They can try to work against a time limit, using an egg-timer or a stop watch.

95

### Activity 9: Spin a sound

This is a difficult exercise and is for children who have learnt many sounds already and can apply them in their own writing. Make a card spinner and divide it into five sections. Write one sound in each section, each in a different colour. Again, these sounds should be ones you have already introduced and wish to reinforce. Small groups can play this game and each player needs a sheet of paper and a pencil. To play, spin the spinner and whatever sound it lands on the player writes down as many words containing that sound as possible. He or she can carry on writing until his/her next turn. Have three turns for each player and then the one with the greatest number of correct words in any one list is the winner.

### Activity 10: Word jumble

Introduce a new sound with discussion, brainstorming and lists of words. Next take ten words from that list and jumble up the order of the letters in the words. Ask the children to rebuild the words by first constructing the 'sound of the moment' and then trying to fit the other letters round it. Organise the children into groups so that they can make jumbled word lists for others to solve and vice versa.

### Activity 11: Crosswords

Crosswords can be produced at several levels of difficulty, the variations being the total number of words and the difficulty of the clues. Make crosswords to

96

Across 1. winter comes after __tumn.
2. I broke a s__cer.

Down 1. The writer of a book is the __thor.
2. Smoke comes from a car's exh__st.
3. I love tomato s__ce.

help teach a sound by using only words which contain the sound you are working on. Use one sound at a time to emphasise its use. The word for the crossword can be part of the clue sentence to put the word in context.

**Activity 12: Game show**
To provide an enjoyable and useful reinforcement of several sounds, have a spelling test in the form of a team competition. Divide the class as seems practical in your situation and use children as the quizmasters and score-keepers. You can dramatise the event by using the same approach as a television game show.

**Copymasters**
Use **copymaster 106** (Crossword) as an example of a more difficult crossword which uses conventional clues but gives the initial letter of the words. This crossword helps to practise use of the vowel combination 'ie'.

Use **copymaster 107** (Sounds check: consonants) to record the children's knowledge of consonant blends. The children can colour in a square when they can read the sound.

# VOWELS AND COMMON LETTER STRINGS

## Purpose
To give the children practice in using vowel sounds and common letter strings.

## Materials needed
General classroom materials.

## Introduction
The general strategy outlined in area of study 1 can be used with the sounds in this area of study. However, a difficulty arises here in the quantity of material to learn. Some vowel sounds and common endings may have been covered at an earlier stage, for example in Key Stage 1, Attainment Target 4, Level 2. They can be revised at this stage. You will probably need a good period of time to present the remaining common sounds. The children's reading may already have given them experience of many of the sounds in use.

*Vowel sounds*     There are five vowel letters in English and each of these can be pronounced as a long or short sound. For example, the short sound as in tub, tap, tip, let, lot and the long sound as in tape, like, tube, he, dope. A dictionary usually indicates if a vowel is short or long so that we know how to pronounce the word.

In addition to this the five vowels can be combined, either with another vowel or with a consonant to produce about twenty vowel sounds used regularly in English. They are:

| | | |
|---|---|---|
| The sound 'a' as in *hat* is usually spelt with an 'a'. | The sound 'aw' as in *dawn* can be spelt:<br>1. 'a' as in *tall*<br>2. 'al' as in *talk*<br>3. 'augh' as in *caught*<br>4. 'aw' as in *paw*<br>5. 'oar' as in *roar*<br>6. 'or' as in *sword*<br>7. 'ough' as in *ought* | The sound 'ee' as in *see* can be spelt:<br>1. 'e' as in *demon*<br>2. 'ea' as in *meat*<br>3. 'ee' as in *tree*<br>4. 'ei' as in *ceiling*<br>5. 'ey' as in *monkey*<br>6. 'i' as in *marine*<br>7. 'ie' as in *field* |
| The sound 'a' as in *gate* can be spelt:<br>1. 'a' as in *mate*<br>2. 'ai' as in *plain*<br>3. 'ay' as in *play*<br>4. 'ea' as in *break*<br>5. 'ei' as in *eight*<br>6. 'ey' as in *grey* | | |
| | The sound 'e' as in *spell* can be spelt:<br>1. 'e' as in *bed*<br>2. 'ea' as in *thread* | The sound 'er' as in *jerk* can be spelt:<br>1. 'er' as in *her*<br>2. 'er' as in *service*<br>3. 'ir' as in *third*<br>4. 'or' as in *word*<br>5. 'our' as in *journey*<br>6. 'ur' as in *purse* |
| The sound 'a' as in *vase* can be spelt:<br>1. 'a' as in *pass*<br>2. 'al' as in *calf*<br>3. 'ar' as in *far*<br>4. 'au' as in *laugh* | | |
| The sound 'air' as in *fair* can be spelt:<br>1. 'air' as in *pair*<br>2. 'are' as in *dare*<br>3. 'ear' as in *bear*<br>4. 'ere' as in *there*<br>5. 'eir' as in *their* | The sound 'ear' as in *disappear* can be spelt:<br>1. 'ear' as in *near*<br>2. 'eer' as in *deer*<br>3. 'ere' as in *here*<br>4. 'ier' as in *wier* | The sound 'i' as in *sit* can be spelt:<br>1. 'i' as in *win*<br>2. 'ui' as in *built*<br>3. 'y' as in *pyramid* |

The sound 'i' as in *drive* can be spelt:
1. 'i' as in *time*
2. 'igh' as in *high*
3. 'ie' as in *tie*
4. 'ye' as in *goodbye*
5. 'y' as in *try*

The sound 'ore' as in *more* can be spelt:
1. 'oor' as in *door*
2. 'our' as in *four*
3. 'ur' as in *fury*
4. 'ure' as in *sure*

The sound 'u' as in *push* can be spelt:
1. 'oo' as in *took*
2. 'ou' as in *could*
3. 'u' as in *full*

The sound 'o' as in *hop* can be spelt:
1. 'a' as in *wasp*
2. 'au' as in *sausage*
3. 'o' as in *trot*
4. 'ou' as in *trough*

The sound 'ow' as in *frown* can be spelt:
1. 'ou' as in *out*
2. 'ow' as in *down*

The sound 'u' ('you') as in *use* can be spelt:
1. 'ew' as in *new*
2. 'u' as in *duty*

The sound 'oy' as in *boy* can be spelt:
1. 'oi' as in *loin*
2. 'oy' as in *joy*

The sound 'o' as in *broke* can be spelt:
1. 'o' as in *tone*
2. 'oa' as in *float*
3. 'oe' as in *toe*
4. 'ow' as in *grow*

The sound 'u' as in *duck* can be spelt:
1. 'o' as in *come*
2. 'ou' as in *young*
3. 'u' as in *lunch*

The sound 'u' as in *rule* can be spelt:
1. 'ew' as in *few*
2. 'o' as in *to*
3. 'oo' as in *zoo*
4. 'ou' as in *soup*
5. 'u' as in *lute*
6. 'ui' as in *fruit*

*Letter strings* These are usually at the ends of words and the most commonly used ones are: ing, ous, ion, ly, le, ies, ied, ed, tch, ves, ful, dge, ought, ight.

In keeping with the first area of study we suggest that you adopt the same working strategy and we offer some activities for helping to teach these sounds.

**Activity 1: A sound web**
To help with the initial brainstorming make a sound web. Pick a word which has the sound in it and is also suitable for illustration. For example if the sound is 'le' then the word 'twinkle' could be illustrated by a star. Using a large piece of paper make a poster as shown

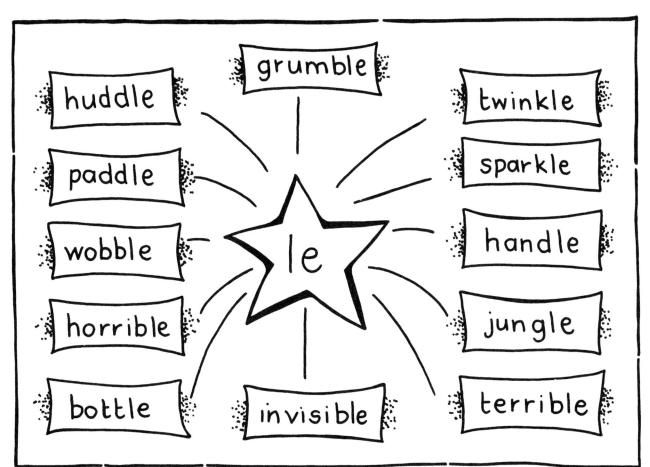

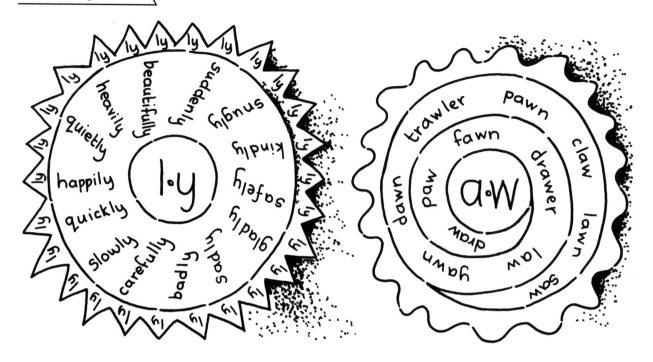

on page 99. As you think of words using this sound, write them, or get the children to take turns writing them around the star and join these words to the star to make a visible connection. This can then be used as a wall poster and *aide-mémoire*.

### Activity 2: Sound spinner
This can be used as a word bank and as a visual aid when introducing the sound. Use a 20 cm circle of stiff cartridge paper or card and draw the sound in a circle in the centre. Write words using the sound round the edge of the circle arranged like spokes in a bicycle wheel. Put a large drawing-pin through the centre and pin the circle in an accessible place so that the children can add to it or consult it by turning it around.

As an alternative, draw a spiral on the circle and write the words around its lines.

### Activity 3: Word slide
To help teach a letter string which comes at the end of a word make the device shown below. Ask the children to write a sentence to show how each word is used or to invent a short passage using as many of the words as possible.

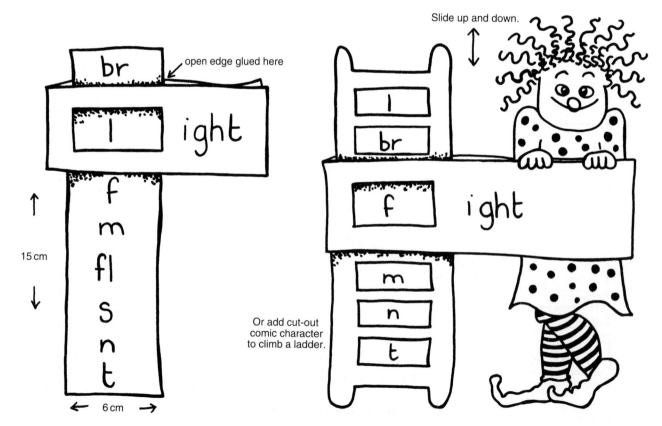

100

## Activity 4: Missing letters

Draw a structure similar to a crossword but write in some of the letters of the words. Give clues as to the identity of the words and use words with the same letter string or sound. Get the children to work in pairs or threes to construct their own missing letter puzzles.

## Activity 5: Jumble match

Make worksheets as follows: write a list of words using the same sound. Next to it write the same list but in a different order and with the letters of the words jumbled up too. Ask the children to match each jumbled word to its correctly written partner. You can add a third column for the children to actually write out the correct version as this often fixes it in their minds more effectively.

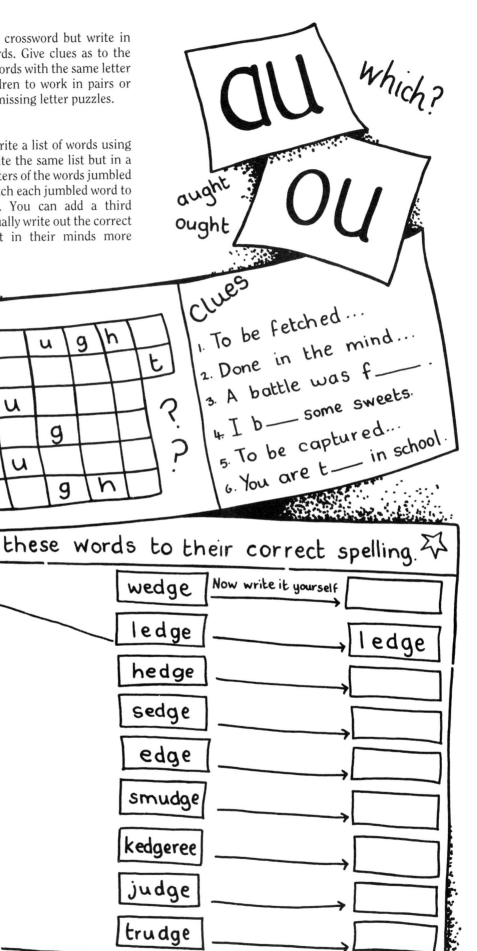

**au  ou**  *which?*

*aught*
*ought*

**Puzzle**

| | | r | | u | g | h | |
| | t | h | | | | | t |
| | f | | u | | | | |
| | b | o | | | g | | |
| | c | a | u | | | | |
| | t | | | | g | h | |

**Clues**

1. To be fetched...
2. Done in the mind...
3. A battle was f____
4. I b____ some sweets.
5. To be captured...
6. You are t____ in school.

### ⭐ Join these words to their correct spelling. ⭐

| | | Now write it yourself |
| edgle | wedge | → ☐ |
| edsge | ledge | → ledge |
| dege | hedge | → ☐ |
| mudsge | sedge | → ☐ |
| ehdge | edge | → ☐ |
| edwge | smudge | → ☐ |
| udgje | kedgeree | → ☐ |
| rudtge | judge | → ☐ |
| ekdgeree | trudge | → ☐ |

**Activity 6: What's the answer?**

In order to put words in context make up a set of questions which require a simple 'yes' or 'no' answer. One word in the sentence should, of course, contain the sound of the moment and that sound can be replaced by the equivalent number of dashes so that the children have to fill it in to complete the word and read the sentence.

You could substitute the questions for a statement which needs a 'true' or 'false' response.

You can also add the missing words and some decoys at the bottom of the card, for reference.

**Activity 7: Endings – jigsaws**

Some letter strings produce endings that change the use of a word but do not change the original word, for example, 'ly', 'ful' and 'ing'. You can present these to the children as a jigsaw image to fix the concept of 'an addition without changing the original word' in their minds. The children have to add the endings to the words by simply matching them. Present them with a passage or sentences which use the words that have just been made. Miss these words out and get the children to add a suitable word to complete the sentence.

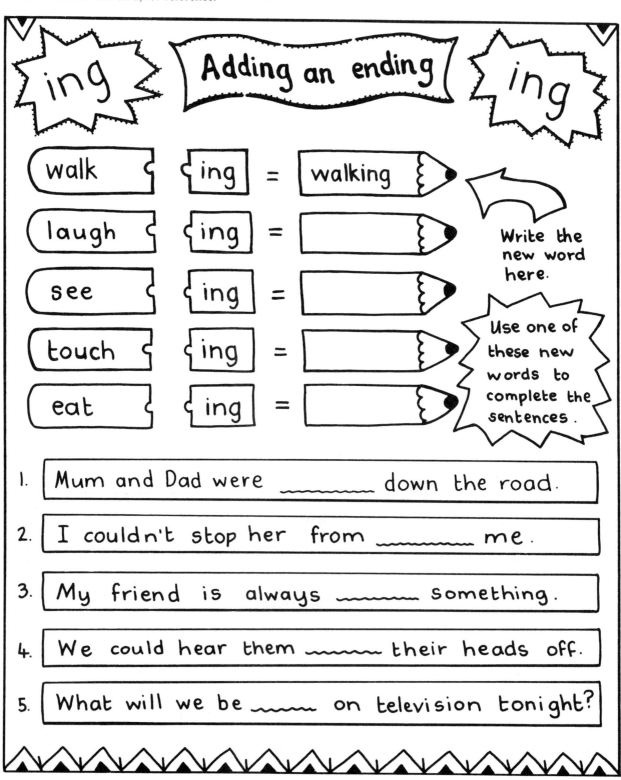

**Adding an ending**

walk { ing = walking

laugh { ing =

see { ing =

touch { ing =

eat { ing =

Write the new word here.

Use one of these new words to complete the sentences.

1. Mum and Dad were _____ down the road.

2. I couldn't stop her from _____ me.

3. My friend is always _____ something.

4. We could hear them _____ their heads off.

5. What will we be _____ on television tonight?

Put in the missing sounds and answer the questions. yes no

1. Would you like to cli__ a fire engine's ladder?
2. Have you got five fingers and one thu__?
3. Are legs and arms called li__s?
4. Is a la__ a young pig?
5. Are you du__?
6. Have you ever been nu__ with cold?

| thumb | numb | dumb | lamb | limb | climb |

**Activity 8: Sound ride**

This is a fairground ride to help children to change spelling according to use. Using thin card make a structure as shown below to help the children see how some words are changed to produce a plural or the past tense, for example, by adding 'ies' or 'ied'. If the children make the line themselves this may help them to remember the spellings too. You could draw a template of the car for them to draw round and they could draw in their own idea of a driver. A figure cut from a newspaper or comic or a photo of the child could be used as the driver. You could help them to make the line as part of a measuring exercise. Get them to convert the words on paper too.

Cover the end of the word with the 'ies' ending.

← slide →

line/track

body | baby | cop | ies | cry | fly | dry

reverse of car

glue

reverse of track with car in place

103

### Activity 9: Sounds scan

This is a game for a group of children. Collect some comics, magazines, newspapers and a timer of some kind. Let each child or pair of children pick a paper. Arm them with a felt pen and ask them to scan the pages and then underline all words which use a certain sound. For instance those having the 'aw' sound or those ending with 'ion'. Make it a race and write all correct words on the board at the end so that you have a set of words using your sound. The children who collected the most correct words are the winners.

### Activity 10: Word maze

This is a simple closed maze, i.e. it has a correct route and several dead ends. It is a useful device for presenting the children with a choice which, in this case, is between the correct or incorrect spelling of a set of words all of which use the same sound combination. The children are given the list of correct spellings for reference to help them pick a route which follows the correctly spelled words.

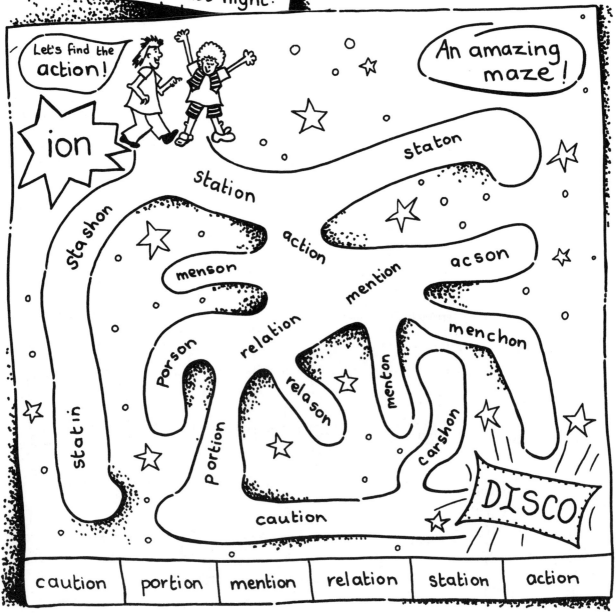

## Copymasters

Use **copymaster 108** (Sounds maze) as a blank for you to write your own selection of words. You can produce your own copymaster by photocopying one sheet, writing on your words and then using this as a master. Repeat the process when you want to use a different set of words to teach another sound. Decorate your own master sheet with illustrations on one theme. For example you may call it a 'Walk through the woods' and draw in trees and animals to make it more appealing for the children.

Use **copymaster 109** (Sounds check: vowels) as a checklist for you or the children to record which vowels or vowel combinations they know.

Use **copymaster 110** (Sounds check: letter strings) as above but this time to record the acquisition of common letter strings.

# WORD FAMILIES

## Purpose

To help the children to identify word families.

## Activity 1: Looking for relationships between words

With the many different words that the children use in the course of their writing, it is as well to try and encourage them to look at the structure of words and to break down the words they need into separate parts which will help them to visualise the word whenever they need it. The 'look, cover, remember, write' strategy is probably the most helpful, since it helps them to:

a) see the word written correctly;
b) form a correct visual image;
c) identify any difficult parts;
d) associate the sound of the word with the usual form of it;
e) try to recall its structure when writing it in future.

With word families the children should try to look for similar words used for different purposes. These are words that have the same basic stem contained in a polysyllabic word. If we take the example given in the National Curriculum document, the word 'grow' can be used in a simple sentence such as: 'I like to grow flowers.' If we wish to write another sentence in a slightly different way the word 'grow' also has to change. Now if we write 'I have grown potatoes in the past' we notice that the word has changed from grow into grown because it is now referring to the past tense. Give the children a set of words and discuss with them the other forms of those words that they might use.

As an extension to this and in order to give the children more opportunity for recognising word families, make some playing cards and play a game like Happy Families. For this all you need to do is write the words that the children suggest on the cards. The children have to keep looking for the words which belong to the same family as the cards they already hold. Share the cards out among a small group of children. The first child starts by asking the person on his/her right if they have another form of one of the words on the cards he/she holds. For example if the first player has 'smiling' on one of his cards he asks the second player if he has a card from the same family. If the second player has got another word from the same family, such as 'smiled', he must had it over but, if he has not, then it is his turn to ask the player on his right and so on. When a child thinks that one particular word family is complete he/she places the cards face down on the table. When all the players think they have completed their families any remaining cards are put on one side. Then the cards are checked to see who has the greatest number of complete families. The left-over cards are also checked and if there are any cards belonging to one of the families that have been claimed as complete then that player does not count that particular word family in his total of complete sets. The player who has the most families is the winner. The great advantage of this game is that it can be as simple or as complex as required by varying the number of word families at any one time.

When the children are used to playing this game and

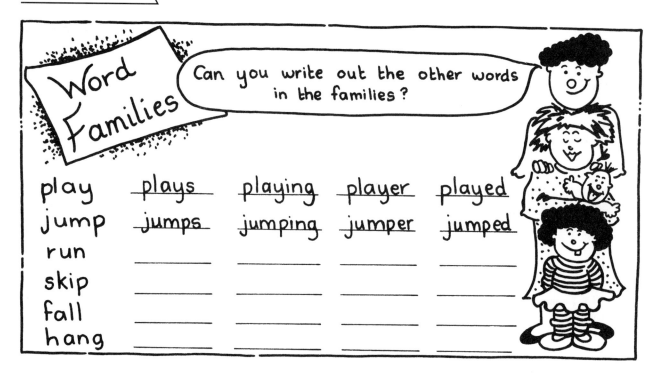

are familiar with the many variations of simple verbs, make some workcards as illustrated on this page.

Choose simple verbs and ask the children to think of as many other members of the same family as they can. There are six spaces on the card but the children need only to fill in as many as they can think of – for some of the words there are only four possible answers. This will give the children more practice in recognising the members of the word families, because when they have finished the cards you can discuss with them any other members of the word family that they may have missed.

Use **copymaster 111** (Word families) for the children to look at the grid containing the members of given word families. They look for the members and colour each member of the same family one colour, then choose a different colour for the members of a different word family. The empty grid at the bottom can be used for making grids of different words, either by the teacher or by the children themselves. These can then be exchanged between the children and used in the same way as before.

**Activity 2: Using the words in context**
Make a set of activity cards where the children have to read the sentence and use the correct word from the word bank.

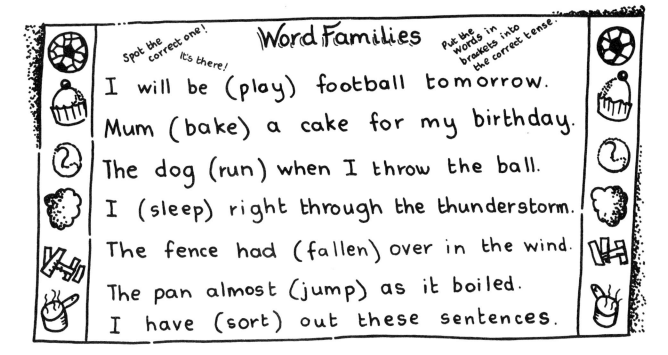

**Word Families**

*Spot the correct one! It's there!*

*Put the words in brackets into the correct tense.*

I will be (play) football tomorrow.

Mum (bake) a cake for my birthday.

The dog (run) when I throw the ball.

I (sleep) right through the thunderstorm.

The fence had (fallen) over in the wind.

The pan almost (jump) as it boiled.

I have (sort) out these sentences.

The children can write out the sentence and be encouraged to look, cover, write and check when they have to choose the right word to make the sentence correct. Give the children lots of practice in this and then ask them to complete sentences without the help of the word bank. For this activity they will need to use the skills derived from the above workcards when choosing the correct tense of the word they need.

They read the sentence and they look at the word in brackets. Then they write out the sentence using the correct tense of the verb so that the sentence makes sense. The children can also look at a variety of texts from their favourite books and look for the verbs contained in them. As they identify the verbs they should write them down and, at the side, try to write the tense as being 'past' (those events which have already happened), 'present' (those events which are happening at the moment), or 'future' (those events which have yet to take place).

Use **copymaster 112** (Tenses) for the children to highlight the verbs. They can use a different colour pen for the different tense. If the verb is in the past tense, underline it in red; the present tense, underline it in green, and the future tense, underline it in blue.

---

**Area of study 4**

# CHECKING SPELLING ▶

**Purpose**

To give the children the opportunity to check spelling using a variety of different resources.

**Activity 1: Using a simple dictionary**

In the process of revising and redrafting the children will need to start working independently in order to check the accuracy of their spelling. They will need to know how to use a dictionary and the first step in acquiring this skill is a knowledge of the position of the letters of the alphabet. The work done at Level 2 in *English Key Stage 1* in this series gives activities for this and, at this level, it is assumed that the children have this knowledge already. All the words in the dictionary are in order of the alphabet so give the children practice in opening the dictionary in roughly the right place for the word they need. They will know, for example, that words beginning with 'a' come at the beginning of the book. Ask them to find the words beginning with 'm'. These are roughly in the middle of the book. Let the children practise opening the book in the right place to find the words beginning with 'm'. Then they can find the words beginning with 'd' which are to be found in the middle of the first half of the dictionary, and then 's' which are found in the middle of the second half of the dictionary. Give lots of practice in this until they are quite used to opening the dictionary in more or less the right section. Now you can ask them to say which letters come first in the alphabet: a or z, n or f, h or p, b or y, s or v, w or c?

This can be extended by asking the children to say which word you would find nearer the beginning of the dictionary; summer or autumn? Obviously, autumn begins with 'a' so that will be nearer to the beginning and you can then ask the children to put a set of words into alphabetical order:

a) grape, apple, pear, orange
b) house, bungalow, castle, palace, mansion
c) dog, rabbit, gerbil, cat, canary, fish, mouse
d) hat, coat, tie, shirt, jacket

You can start to give the children practice in finding words in the dictionary now. If you have a set of class dictionaries, give the children a list of words each beginning with a different letter of the alphabet and ask them to write the page number where it can be found. Extend this activity by giving the children words with the same initial letter such as 'beef' and 'butterfly'. To find these words they will need to find the section of the book containing words beginning with 'b'. Now, instead of starting at the beginning and going through all the words under 'b', they can use their knowledge of the alphabet by looking at the second letter in the word 'beef'; 'e' is nearer to the beginning of the alphabet than the second letter of the word 'butterfly' which is 'u' so it follows that the word 'beef' will be near the beginning of the 'b' section and the word 'butterfly' will be nearer the end. With practice the children will be able to find the words they need quickly and they can take it in turns to test their friends by asking them to find a particular word and see who is the first to find it.

### Activity 2: Spelling books and word banks
The children can make their own spelling books where they use the look, cover, write and check approach. The pages of the spelling book should be marked with columns as shown here and the cover of the book should have an extension to it so that it can be used to cover the word written by the teacher.

A child asks the teacher how to spell a word he or she needs and the teacher writes it down. The child then looks carefully at the word and folds over the extension flap so that he or she cannot see the word the teacher has written. The child tries to write the word him/herself and then checks it against the original. The provision of a work bank can foster even more independence in the children since they will not need to wait for a word to be spelt if the teacher or other adult is busy. The word bank can be set up as in the illustration and the children look for the wallet with the initial letter of the word(s) they need.

They can look at the card for the word, turn the card over and then try to write the word from memory. Next they check it by looking at the card once more and, if it is still incorrect, repeat the process until it is correct.

### Activity 3: Using a spelling checker
Children's spelling often improves when they use word processors and spelling checkers. This is because the incorrect spellings can be identified more easily when they are displayed on the screen or on a print-out than when the children have written them by hand. Also the words can be deleted and replaced more easily, so the children actually like to identify and correct the errors. Another reason is that the children see the public nature of writing and so they are more motivated to make sure that their spellings are correct. The use of a spelling checker will largely be dependent upon the availability of a computer/word processor and the range of software individual schools have. It is also important to remember that when using a spelling checker not all the words are identified as being misspelled. One of the reasons is that spelling checkers cannot take into account the context, so if a child writes 'I like to come my hair', the spelling checker will not identify the word 'come' as wrong and needing to be replaced by 'comb', because 'come' itself was spelled correctly. The spelling checker cannot identify that the word is incorrect in that sentence. A very good and relatively cheap spelling checker is Edspell. This can be used to check text produced with most word processors such as Wordwise, View, Edword, Desktop, its own editor and most other BBC word processors. It is produced by LTS. Another

good program is Predictype which helps speed the rate of text creation and, above all, helps with checking the accuracy of spelling. The program learns with its users so that personalised dictionaries on discs can be created for each. The word processors supported are Wordwise, Wordwise Plus, View and Writer. Full details of these and other programs can be found in the AVP Catalogue, the address of which is on page 89. Individual hand-held spelling checkers are available but the cost is usually prohibitive for purchase in large numbers for use in schools. Individual children may have been given them as presents and may bring them into school from home so that others can try them. On-line dictionaries enable the writer to type in a word and obtain its dictionary entry on screen, but most school computers are not yet powerful enough to accommodate this facility. Nevertheless it is an indication of the way things are moving and, in years to come, many more exciting possibilities will become apparent.

# Attainment target 4: Spelling

| Level 4 | **Statements of attainment** | **Example** |
|---|---|---|
| | Pupils should be able to: | |
| | a) spell correctly, in the course of their own writing, words which display other main patterns in English spelling. | *Words using the main prefixes and suffixes.* |

 **Area of study 1**

# PREFIXES AND SUFFIXES

 C113 –114

## Purpose
To give the children the opportunity to practise use of prefixes and suffixes.

## Materials needed
General classroom materials.

## Prefixes
A prefix is a group of letters which can be added to the front of a word to change the meaning, but it does not change the spelling of that word. English is full of exceptions to the rule and, in this case, they are the prefixes 'well' and 'all' because when they are added to the front of other words they have only one 'l', as in 'altogether'. Prefixes have their own meanings – most of them have their origins in Latin or Greek – and knowledge of these meanings can help to analyse the meaning and spelling of many English words.

## Activity 1: Dictionary research
Get the children to use dictionaries to look up the common prefixes and their meanings. They can then look up a few examples of some prefixes. The common prefixes are shown on the chart adjacent.

Alternatively, you can give the children a number of prefixes and ask them to find five examples of each in the dictionary. Most dictionaries do list prefixes as main entry words. It is important that the children read the dictionary definition carefully to ascertain that the initial sound is indeed a prefix.

| *Common prefixes* | *Meanings* |
|---|---|
| ab | away from |
| ad | to, towards |
| ante | before |
| anti | against |
| bi | two |
| com | together, with |
| de | removal of, reversal of, departure from |
| dia | through, across |
| en/in | in |
| epi | upon, above |
| ex | out of, away, former |
| hyper | above, greater, in excess |
| hypo | below, lesser |
| inter | between, together |
| mal | bad |
| mono | single, one |
| per | through, throughout |
| poly | more than one, many |
| post | after, behind |
| pro | in favour of, substitute for, before, forward |
| re | again, back |
| sub | below, less than |
| super/sur | over, beyond |
| syn | with, together |
| tele | far away |
| tri | three |
| uni | one |

As another exercise, get the children to look up words beginning with the prefixes of quantity, such as mono, uni, bi, tri, poly and to write down as many words as they can find under each one. Use different editions of dictionaries in case of variation.

### Activity 2: Make a dictionary of prefixes
Using an indented notebook, list the prefixes in alphabetical order, with a suitable illustration on the initial page if possible. Then add examples to the

dictionary as a result of the research above or during the course of other work in the day.

### Activity 3: Opposites
A prefix can be added to give the opposite meaning to a word. The following negative prefixes are quite common: dis, in, mis, non, un. Give the children a list of words and ask them to add the negative prefixes to give the opposite meaning, or ask them to take away the prefix to give the opposite meaning.

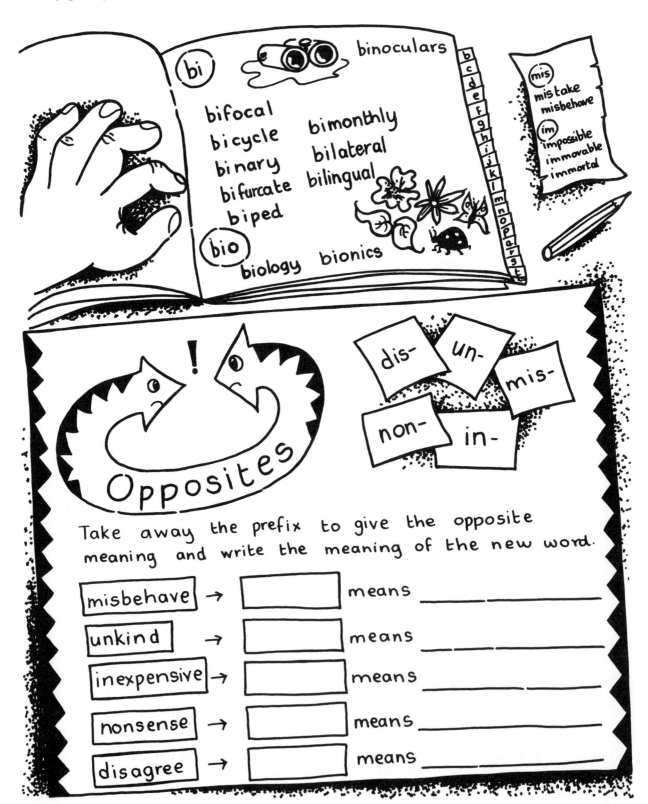

**Activity 4: Meanings**
Give the children a list of words with prefixes and ask them to write down what the prefix means.

| word | prefix | meaning |
|---|---|---|
| submerge | sub | below |
| malformation | mal | bad, faulty |
| bifocal | bi | two |
| illegal | il | against |
| telescope | tele | |
| antiseptic | anti | |
| displease | dis | |

## Pick a prefix
Add the correct prefix to these words.

**dis or de**
obedient
comfort
hydrate
lay

**pre or pro**
caution
historic
molar
noun

**im or il**
possible
movable
mortal
legal
logical

**dis or mis**
understand
take
agree
please

**un or in**
reliable
screw
roll
effective
expensive

**Activity 5: Adding the right one**
Make worksheets as shown above for the children to choose the correct prefix to go with a word. They can use a dictionary.

Use **copymaster 113** (Prefixes) to give the children practice in using prefixes and spelling them correctly.

111

**Suffixes**

A suffix is a group of letters added to the end of a word to change the way the word is used as a part of speech. For example in this sentence, 'Bessie was eating the buns', the suffix 'ing' was added to the verb 'eat'. However in this sentence, 'Bessie is a champion eater', the suffix 'er' is added to 'eat' to make it into a noun. The spelling rules governing the addition of suffixes are varied and complicated. The suffix never changes but the spelling of the word to which it is added often does. We feel these complex rules are too difficult at this level.

In Level 3 (p.102) some examples of common suffixes were included. There is also a selection of activities which can be used to give children practice in spelling and using words with these endings. It was suggested that the spelling patterns be taught by presenting the children with groups of words used in a context and by asking the children to recognise, write and use those words. The method does rely on memory to a certain extent but provides context clues to jog the memory. The 'look, cover, write and check' procedure as a spelling strategy is very good at all levels.

Here are the common suffixes and their uses.

| Common suffixes | | |
| --- | --- | --- |
| *a) used to form nouns* | | |
| er | ly | ance |
| or | hood | ence |
| ar | ness | ment |
| re | ism | ice |
| ship | ure | age |
| *b) used to form adjectives* | | |
| ary | ish | ic |
| ery | less | like |
| ory | ly | y |
| en | ous | ful |
| *c) used to end verbs* | | |
| ing | ure | ize |
| ed | ise | yse |
| ude | | |

Add suffixes to the incomplete words to make them correct.

Quiet_ and quick_ the glisten__ snake glide_ down from the high __ branches. It hung clever_ in midair for a moment then turn__ deft_ it disappear_ into the cool foliage.

112

**Activity 6: Changed words**
Write or copy a descriptive passage but put a selection of the verbs, adjectives and adverbs in the wrong tense and ask the children to correct them by adding suitable suffixes.

**Activity 7: I-spy**
Give the children a passage of writing or a list of words and ask them to underline all the prefixes and suffixes. Do one exercise as a class activity first and go through it as a group to check their findings.

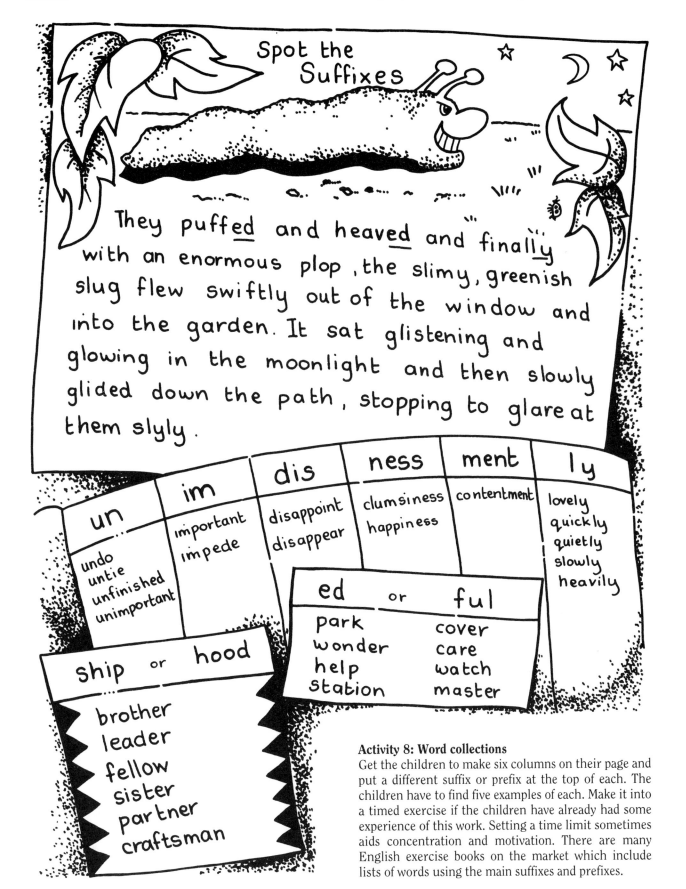

Spot the Suffixes

They puff<u>ed</u> and heav<u>ed</u> and finall<u>y</u> with an enormous plop, the slimy, greenish slug flew swiftly out of the window and into the garden. It sat glistening and glowing in the moonlight and then slowly glided down the path, stopping to glare at them slyly.

| un | im | dis | ness | ment | ly |
|---|---|---|---|---|---|
| | important | disappoint | clumsiness | contentment | lovely |
| | impede | disappear | happiness | | quickly |
| undo | | | | | quietly |
| untie | | | | | slowly |
| unfinished | | | | | heavily |
| unimportant | | | | | |

| ed | or | ful |
|---|---|---|
| park | | cover |
| wonder | | care |
| help | | watch |
| station | | master |

| ship | or | hood |
|---|---|---|
| brother | | |
| leader | | |
| fellow | | |
| sister | | |
| partner | | |
| craftsman | | |

**Activity 8: Word collections**
Get the children to make six columns on their page and put a different suffix or prefix at the top of each. The children have to find five examples of each. Make it into a timed exercise if the children have already had some experience of this work. Setting a time limit sometimes aids concentration and motivation. There are many English exercise books on the market which include lists of words using the main suffixes and prefixes.

**Activity 9: Keep changing**

Make four columns on the page and, in the first column, write about six words that can be changed by having a prefix, a suffix or both of these added to them. Ask the children to add appropriate suffixes and prefixes to the rest of the words and include a few more examples of their own.

Use **copymaster 114** (Suffixes) which contains several exercises to give the children practice in the use of suffixes.

| Word | Prefix added | Suffix added | Both added |
|---|---|---|---|
| kind | unkind | kindness | unkindness |
| love | unloved | lovely | unlovely |
| happy | unhappy | happiness | unhappiness |
| honest | dishonest | honesty | dishonesty |
| safe | unsafe | safety | unsafely |
| tidy | untidy | tidiness | untidiness |
| fasten | unfasten | fastened | unfastened |

# ATTAINMENT TARGET 5: Handwriting

## Attainment target 5: Handwriting

| Level 3 | **Statements of attainment** |
|---|---|

Pupils should be able to:

a) begin to produce clear and legible joined-up writing.

---

## INTRODUCING JOINED-UP WRITING

C115 –123

---

### Purpose
To introduce ligatures for joining letters together.

### Activity 1: The families of joins
It is important to remember that children do need to be able to form their letters correctly if they are going to join them in the correct and most fluent way. Providing enough initial training has been done in the movement of letters so that the children form their letters properly and comfortably, the first step is the addition of exit strokes on all the letters that terminate at the base line. It is very difficult to come down on the side of any particular approach to the teaching of the skills of handwriting since there is a great diversity of material currently being used in schools. To highlight one particular style or method would mean neglecting the others, so it is intended to give a general set of activities which may be adapted to a school's particular needs and chosen style of handwriting. Schools must decide their own policy for joins. Some insist that every letter be joined and therefore this means incorporating looped descenders. Others adopt a policy of 'join when comfortable'. Whichever is decided upon, the children should be given an opportunity to discuss it so that they can understand what is expected of them and how the joins can help to make their writing flow more easily.

Many schools start off by giving the children practice in making continuous patterns on paper with a pencil or a felt tip pen, to help them to get the idea of smooth flowing movements.

Left hand

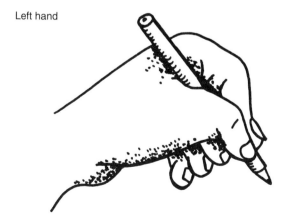

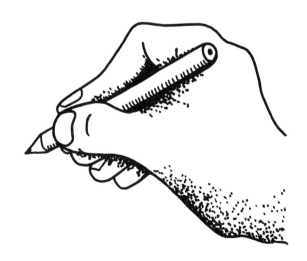

**Grip the pencil lightly between the first finger and thumb. The second finger is used as a 'cushion' underneath the pencil. Rest the hand and arm on a table. Let the pencil rest on the hand between the base of the first finger and thumb.**

Right hand

**Sit facing the table with elbows and arms resting on the table. Keep all fingers, apart from the first finger, underneath the pencil. The pencil end should point over the shoulder on the same side.**
**Use the 'free' hand to hold the paper steady.**

Use **copymaster 115** (Patterns 1) and **copymaster 116** (Patterns 2) to give the children practice in sitting comfortably, holding the pencil properly and feeling the smooth flow of the pencil over the paper. Remember to repeat the pattern only for as long as is comfortable without lifting the pencil off the paper.

When the children have had much experience of this it is time to introduce the families of joins. The following letters all join spontaneously at the base line.

iltuhnmacdek
iltuhnmacdek

The letter 'f' can join from the crossbar and the letter 't' can also join in the same way.

f f t t    forget
tomorrow
tomorrow

The letters 'o', 'r', 'v', and 'w' all join from the top.

orvw    orvw

The joins to these letters: 'a', 'c', 'd', 'g', 'o', 'q' all go over the top and back.

acdgoq
acdgoq

With the next set of letters: 'g', 'j', 'y', 'q', the first three letters can be left unjoined or a loop can be made from the descender. The join for 'q' is not like any other join and should be taught separately.

gjyq    gjyq
jgjg    qgqg

116

For the final set of letters: 'p', 'b', 'x', 'z', 's', the 'p' and 'b' can be joined or not, as preferred; the letters 'x' and 'z' are probably better left unjoined; and 's' is often left unjoined if it starts a word and looks better if it is kept very simple when it is written in the middle of words or when there are two side by side.

b p play play
big big big
x z box zoo
dresses dresses
sometimes

When the children are joining to tall letters remind them that they do not join right at the top. A good practice point is for the children to take off their pencil at the end of an upstroke and take it quickly to the top of the tall letter. The downward stroke of the tall letter will join the two letters together very well. Give the children practice in joining the pairs of letter so that they get used to moving the pencil quickly and smoothly between the upstroke and the beginning of the next letter.

ab if if eh ck
ef ef uk th ib
at il ul nt it

### Activity 2: Writing letters together

Give the children practice in joining sets of different letters together until they can make the joins quickly, smoothly and correctly. The letters 'a', 'c', 'd', 'e', 'h', 'i', 'k', 'l', 'm', 'n', 't' and 'u' all finish with an upstroke so they can easily be joined to the beginning of the letters 'e', 'i', 'j', 'm', 'n', 'p', 'r', 'u', 'v', 'w', 'x' and 'y' as shown.

en ar ai ee
me er um ce
li hi he de
tu te cu ev
ey ar tr ay
di un in ie

The children can then write words like these in order to give them further practice in joining the different sets of letters.

hill then silk
thank lift mill
hen tank lank
link kettle call
chilly letter milk
clock think tell

One of the most difficult joins is to oval letters. There are two approaches to this problem, the first is reverse joins and many people think that this promotes flow, but not all children find it easy. For those who have no difficulty, the letter combinations of the 'cacaca', 'cococo', 'cdcdcd', 'agagag', are easy. For those who have difficulty, the alternative approach is once again to use a pencil lift between the end of the up-stroke and the beginning of the oval letter like this:

i     ic     na

Give the children practice in writing the following pairs of letters with a pencil lift between the letters of each pair.

ic ea no ad ig

ma ha id eg ad

ac ca cd co na

nc eq iq do

Let them make patterns with the joins between oval letters to help them to produce them smoothly, quickly and well.

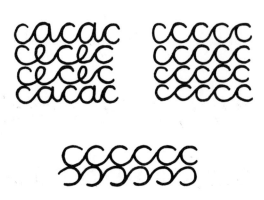

Ask them to try to write pairs of letters quickly with their eyes closed and then they can try writing whole words.

cab touch lace

mace ace cage

dance each beach

teach magic made

Another form of join is the cross join from the letters 'o', 'v' and 'w'. They are formed in the following way:

ooooo     vvvvv

wwww     ooooo

vvvvv     wwww

oi on ou ov oy

ow vi vu vy wi

wn wy vo

118

Cross joins to oval letters can be difficult for some children so it is a good idea to practise these as well, and then try writing whole words quickly and correctly.

*oa od og oo oc*

*wo wa wd wc wg*

*vo vc vg va vq*

*wood our wipe*

*voice only ogre*

*woman moat over*

*viper void voile*

*wide want will*

In many schemes 'o', 'v' and 'w' do not join to tall letters or to 'e', 's' or 'z'.

The letter 'f' is represented in different ways according to the handwriting scheme used. The three most common forms are:

*f f f f f*

With all of these forms the next letter usually joins from the crossbar.

*flower*

*fix    future*

The crossbar then joins onto other letters in the same way that the cross joins connect on 'o', 'v' and 'w'.

In some schemes the letters 'g', 'j' and 'y' do not connect at all unless their descenders incorporate loops. Where they do follow this rule the loops join on to the next letter in the same way as those which join from the base line.

*give gone glue*

*jump jelly join*

*yes  young*

*anything*

The joining of letter 'r' is dealt with separately since, although it does have a cross join as in the letters 'o', 'v' and 'w', in some schemes it does not join to 'e', 's' or 'z'. It is sometimes difficult for the children to write at first so give them lots of practice writing the letter and then try the pairs of letters and the words.

*rrrrrr  rrrrrr*

*ri ru ry rg rc*

*rd rp rq rm rn*

*rose rapid ride*

*road rule ready*

*real flowers furze*

119

ppppp  bbbbb  pbpbp
po pi plo pu pa pd pe
bi bo by ba bl bu be

In many schemes the letters 'p' and 'b' do not join; this is a matter of preference. If a join is required, however, it is simple enough to make the join from the base line.

peck  pump  pick

paint  point  boil

big  blue  bus  beg

The letters 'x' and 'z' are better not joined since they can become difficult to recognise in the middle of words and the letter 's' should be kept as simple as possible when contained in a word, for the same reason. Some schemes do allow the letter to be joined from the base line of certain letters and as a cross join from others. As a rule, it is best not to join the last letter where 'ss' occurs, and to keep the letter separate when the letter 's' begins the word.

box fox express extra zoo

zip zebra fuzz fizzing buzz

fussy past ghost some success

This completes the families of joins and the children will need lots of practice in their writing sessions. Remember to be supportive in the transition stage and keep a watchful eye for any really bad habits forming. Once learned they are very difficult to correct. Try not to inhibit the development of personal style and it is recommended that the children's own copybooks offer a much more flexible approach than an over formal and too rigid scheme. Once the basic structure of the joining of letters has been understood, it will be easy for a more individual style to be developed if wished. For further reading, *Handwriting, the way to teach it* by Rosemary Sassoon is an excellent book, available from Stanley Thornes (Publishers) Ltd.

The following copymasters give practice in joining the whole range of letters.

Use **copymasters 117–122** (Joining letters 1–6) for practice sheets in joining common letter groups.

Use **copymaster 123** (Other letters) for practising exceptions to the rule of joining. The examples given on this sheet are used in some handwriting schemes and not in others. Individuals will have to decide whether these are to be used with their pupils. A separate sheet can be created for any one of the sets of letters by photocopying the whole sheet and then cutting out the part required and pasting it onto another blank sheet.

## Attainment target 5: Handwriting

Level 4

### Statements of attainment

Pupils should be able to:

a) produce more fluent joined-up writing in independent work.

---

Area of study 1 — **FLUENT JOINED-UP WRITING**  C124

### Purpose
To allow the children to use the skills learned at the previous level in order to enable them to write more fluently.

### Activity 1: Using the skills in independent work
As the children produce independent work it will be necessary to observe and assess their progress in using the skills from the previous levels. Provided the formation of letters is correct, the joins should cause little difficulty. In the process of revising and redrafting the children can be encouraged to notice any mistakes they might have made with joining the letters and, if necessary, give them further practice in joining by revising the copymasters from Level 3. A good check on accuracy, style and speed, is to give the children a short passage to copy out in a given time. Encourage them to think of this in a positive way as an aid to developing fluency and speed. A further activity is for the children to check each other's writing and discuss between themselves any alterations that may be necessary.

### Copymasters
Use **copymaster 124** (Writing practice) for the children to practise writing using the lines for guidance. The bold black lines should be used for tall letters and capital letters. The dotted line should be used as a guide when writing lowercase letters to ensure a uniform height. The sheet can also be used for testing the children's accuracy and speed by getting them to copy a short passage from a book or from their own writing in a given amount of time.

121

# Attainment target 4/5: Presentation

| Level 5 | Statements of attainment | Example |
|---|---|---|
| | Pupils should be able to: | |
| | a) spell correctly, in the course of their own writing, words of greater complexity. | *Words with inflectional suffixes, such as -ed and -ing, where consonant doubling ('running') or -e deletion ('coming') are required.* |
| | b) check final drafts of writing for misspelling and other errors of presentation. | *Use a dictionary or computer spelling checker when appropriate.* |
| | c) produce clear and legible handwriting in printed and cursive styles. | |

The work suggested by the statements of attainment for this level has already been covered in some depth at earlier levels and we feel that Level 5 in the primary school should be used as a period of consolidation.